KITCHEN MEETS GIRL

"This book is going to change lives! I have been a fan of Ashley's blog, *Kitchen Meets Girl*, for a long time! Her gorgeous photography and simple recipes always keep me coming back for more. This book is filled with mouth-watering recipes that will appeal to anyone—regardless of cooking experience! Ashely has a way of making a recipe accessible to the everyday cook. The instructions are concise and easy to follow. I wish I had this book when I started out. Regardless I cannot wait to dive in and start cooking!"

— Tanya Schroeder, founder and creator of popular blog *Lemons for Lulu*

Ashley Whitmore

KITCHEN MEETS GIRL

30 EASY MEALS for RELUCTANT COOKS

FRONT TABLE BOOKS | AN IMPRINT OF CEDAR FORT, INC. | SPRINGVILLE, UTAH

ISBN 13: 978-1-4621-1680-5

Published by Front Table Books, an imprint of Cedar Fort, Inc.
2373 W. 700 S., Springville, UT 84663
Distributed by Cedar Fort, Inc., www.cedarfort.com

LIBRARY OF CONGRESS CATALOGING-IN-PUBLICATION DATA

Whitmore, Ashley, 1976-
Kitchen meets girl : 30 easy meals for reluctant cooks / Ashley Whitmore.
     pages cm
Includes index.
ISBN 978-1-4621-1680-5 (acid-free paper)
1. Quick and easy cooking. I. Title.
TX833.5.W493 2015
641.5'12--dc23
                                    2015013617

Cover and page design by M. Shaun McMurdie
Cover design © 2015 by Lyle Mortimer
Edited by Melissa J. Caldwell

Printed in China

10 9 8 7 6 5 4 3 2 1

Printed on acid-free paper

For Deacon

I love you to the moon and back
times infinity

And for Trinity

Thank you for being my biggest champion

"Sit down and feed and welcome to our table."

WILLIAM SHAKESPEARE
from *As You Like It*
Act 2, Scene 7

Contents

Key

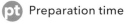 Preparation time   Cook time   Servings/Yield   Freeze time   ct Chill time

Acknowledgments

I couldn't have written this book without a number of people.

First and foremost my husband, Trinity: so very many thanks. You believed in me when I didn't believe in myself, and you gave me the confidence and the courage to chase after my dream. I could not have done this without you. Thank you for listening to me freak out about deadlines, recipe selections, and photography composition. Thank you for eating cold dinners, or dinner foods at 11:00 a.m., and running to the grocery store for emergency ingredients or props.

But mostly, thank you for doing all of those dishes. Holy cow.

To my Doodlebug. Thank you for being so patient with Mommy during all of those weekends I spent in the kitchen and in front of the computer. You're a rock-star kid—you know that, right? I'm so lucky to get to be your mom.

To my parents, who have always been my number one fans. You were the first readers of my blog, the first ones who told me I could do this cookbook thing, the first ones who told me I could do—or be—whatever I wanted in life.

Introduction

It's Monday night. I've just finished a hectic day of work and picked my kiddo up from school. In between trying to complete homework and rushing over to karate practice (or is tonight soccer practice? Swimming lessons? Baseball? I think you get my drift here), I've got to try to figure out what kind of healthy dinner to get on the table.

And fast.

Here's the deal: I didn't grow up in the kitchen, and I had no interest in learning how to cook until I started a family of my own. My mother probably wants me to tell you it was my plan when I was in graduate school to marry a man who knew how to cook so that I didn't have to. Since that didn't happen, and I didn't want to live on Hamburger Helper for the rest of my days, I started experimenting in the kitchen— and logging my successes on my blog back in 2011.

What I've learned about cooking over the years is that anyone can do it. A recipe doesn't have to be complicated, or time-consuming, or use hard-to-find ingredients to make a meal that is family friendly or crowd pleasing. In fact, it's usually just the opposite!

Another thing I've learned over the years is that meal planning is essential for managing your busy days. While it might be easier to swing through the drive-through after work to pick up dinner, or open up one of those box dinners from the grocery stores, neither of those options nourishes our bodies or fosters high-quality family time.

While I think regular family dinners are important, they shouldn't be another stressful check box on your already busy day's list. If you're like me you're doing good to figure out what to make for a main course, let alone trying to come up with some sice dishes other than plain ol' rice and a bag of salad. I can't be the only one who feels this way, right? Can I?

So I started compiling some meal plans to help make my life a little easier—and hopefully yours too. While these are a great starting off point, that doesn't mean you can't mix and match!

These pages are filled with some of my family's favorite recipes, from main dishes like World's Best Chicken Pie (page 37) to Easy Weeknight Chili (page 115) to side dishes, including Perfectly Seasoned Black Beans (page 88), Rosemary Parmesan Roasted Potatoes (page 92), and my Grandma's Oatmeal Rolls (page 128). Of course, no cookbook would be complete without a few desserts—my very favorites are the Individual No-Bake Cherry Cheesecakes (page 125) and the No Churn Strawberry Cheesecake Ice Cream (page 59) running a close second. Clearly, I have a thing for cheesecake.

Whatever your family's tastes, I truly hope the recipes and tips in this book help make your mealtimes a little easier and less hectic.

Successes from my kitchen to yours! – *Ashley*

Tips for Making Mealtime a Success

1. **It probably goes without saying, but meal planning is the number one element in ensuring your mealtimes are successful and stress free!** Find a time each week to meal plan for the upcoming week. Knowing what you are going to make ahead of time allows you to prepare by having ingredients on hand and letting food thaw if needed. Look at your calendar and mark off your busiest nights—those are usually the nights I put my slow cooker to work.

2. **Focus on building a core recipe base of about twenty recipes for each season**—in other words, a group of recipes that your family loves. If you know exactly what you are going to make for your meals and you don't have to search for recipes, you won't end up buying extra ingredients that you won't use. Also, making seasonal recipes decreases costs because you purchase produce at a better price when they are in season.

3. **Before you get started, make sure your kitchen tools (see inset for my list of essential kitchen tools) are handy, your sink is empty, and your countertops are clean.**

4. **The first time you try a new recipe, always read it all the way through before you start cooking.** You don't want to discover that your chicken needs to marinate for *four hours* when you need dinner on the table in *thirty minutes*.

5. **Set all of your ingredients out on the counter before you start cooking.** There's nothing worse than getting halfway

through dinner prep than realizing you're out of diced tomatoes (I'm speaking from personal experience here).

6. **Always follow the recipe exactly the first time you make it.** After that, feel free to modify it to your family's personal preferences.

7. **When it comes to ingredients, fresh is always best.** As you read through the ingredients on the following pages, you'll notice many of them contain citrus juice. Don't skimp here and use the juice from those squeeze bottles—you can definitely taste the difference! If the recipe calls for just half a lemon or a lime, slice up the remainder of the fruit and use it to jazz up your tea or water.

8. **The same goes for herbs**—not much beats the flavor of fresh cilantro, rosemary, thyme, sage, and so forth. You can typically purchase a large bunch of cilantro for around one dollar, but rosemary and thyme (among others) are often a little pricier. If your recipe calls for just a small amount, freeze the rest. Finely chop your leftover herbs and place them in ice cube trays, filling them halfway. Add olive oil to each compartment, filling nearly to the top. Cover with plastic wrap and freeze overnight. Once the cubes have set, pop out of the trays and place in a plastic freezer bag. Mark each bag with the date and contents. Return the bags to the freezer and use the herb cubes within six months.

9. **Relax and have fun!**

Ashley's Essential Kitchen Tools

The recipes in this book use everyday kitchen tools. Here's what you'll need to get dinner on the table.

1. **Cookware.** Small and large nonstick skillets, small and large saucepans, and a stockpot or Dutch oven.

2. **Knives.** While you can get away with less expensive items in most areas, one area you don't want to skimp in is knives—buy the best ones you can afford. You really only need three: a serrated knife, a large chef's knife, and a paring knife.

3. **Cutting boards.** You'll want at least two: one for raw meats and one for cooked foods and produce to avoid cross-contamination.

4. **Utensils.** Heat resistant nonstick spatulas, whisks, wooden spoons, slotted spoons, tongs, and soup ladle.

5. **A set of three stainless steel bowls.** These nesting bowls are inexpensive, versatile, space-saving, and will last forever.

6. **Measuring cups and spoons.** You'll want one set of spoons and two sets of cups. One set of the cups should have handles. These cups should have a pour spout and will be used for measuring liquids. The other set will be used for measuring dry ingredients and can be leveled off.

7. **Bakeware.** A 9 x 13 baking dish, a 3-quart baking dish (or an 8 x 8 baking dish), baking sheets, and a pizza pan.

8. **Slow Cooker.** This is my favorite kitchen appliance. These come in all sizes, so find one that best suits the size of your family. Most come with programmable options now, which I love. This way, my meal does not dry cut or overcook if I don't get home as early as I anticipate.

9. **Electric mixer and blender/food processor.** Blenders have a multitude of uses from chopping to pureeing and are usually much more economical than food processors.

INGREDIENTS:

1 lb. boneless chicken breasts

2 bell peppers, quartered

1 red onion, sliced in thick rings (do not separate rings)

2 tsp. oil

MARINADE:

¼ cup vegetable oil

⅓ cup lime juice (approximately 3 limes)

3 garlic cloves, minced

1 jalapeño, seeded and minced

1 Tbsp. minced fresh cilantro

2 Tbsp. soy sauce

2 Tbsp. liquid smoke

1 tsp. salt

¾ tsp. pepper

FOR SERVING: shredded cheese or queso blanco, pico de gallo, salsa, sour cream, cilantro

Best Ever Fajitas

 30 minutes   15 minutes **S** Serves 4

Skip going out for restaurant fajitas and make your own at home instead! We love cooking these on our outdoor grill, but you can easily make them inside using a grill pan or a large skillet. Whatever you do, don't skip the liquid smoke in this recipe—it's what makes these fajitas extra special.

INSTRUCTIONS:

1. Place chicken in a large resealable bag or a container with a lid and the bell peppers and onion in a second bag or container.

2. Whisk together the marinade ingredients. Reserve 4 tablespoons of the marinade. With the remaining mixture, add a generous splash to the bag containing the vegetables. Add the rest to the bag containing the chicken. Seal the bags, pressing out all of the air, and place bags on a rimmed baking sheet in the refrigerator (in case the bags leak) and allow to marinate for at least 15 minutes, turning once halfway through.

3. When you are ready to cook your chicken, heat oil in a heavy bottomed skillet or grill pan over medium-high heat. Cook chicken until brown on both sides, 5–7 minutes. Reduce heat and continue cooking until cooked through. Remove from pan and tent with foil to keep warm.

4. Place vegetables in the skillet and sauté until tender. Return chicken to pan and warm through.

5. When ready to serve, slice chicken into ¼-inch pieces and slice peppers and onions into strips. Drizzle with remaining tablespoons of marinade.

INGREDIENTS:

3 cups diced tomatoes*

1 (10-oz.) can diced tomatoes with green chilies

2 garlic cloves, minced

1 jalapeño, quartered and diced (seeded if you prefer a milder salsa)

½ cup cilantro, roughly chopped

½ cup diced red onion

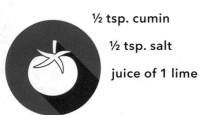

½ tsp. cumin

½ tsp. salt

juice of 1 lime

Better-than-Restaurant Salsa

 15 minutes   n/a   4 cups

Making your own salsa at home takes only a few minutes—plus, you can control the heat and consistency. We like ours thick and spicy, but if you don't, you may substitute the jalapeño with a 4-oz. can of green chilies. Make sure to refrigerate the salsa for an hour before digging in—the flavors deepen over time.

INSTRUCTIONS:

1. Combine ingredients in a blender or food processor, and pulse until you get the consistency you like. For a thick salsa, 6–7 pulses should do the trick. If you prefer a thinner salsa, pulse 10–15 times.

2. Refrigerate for at least an hour before serving.

   * *Since we prefer chunky salsa, I use Roma tomatoes due to their low-moisture flesh.*

INGREDIENTS:

8 frozen strawberries

¼ cup fresh lime juice (about 2 limes)

½ cup fresh lemon juice (about 2 large lemons)

¾ cup lemon-lime soda

⅓–½ cup sugar

4 cups ice

Breezy Strawberry Mocktails

 15 minutes   n/a **S** Serves 4-6

Make every Taco Tuesday (or Fajita Friday) a party with these fun and festive drinks! They are the perfect beverages for entertaining and are super easy to make.

INSTRUCTIONS:

1. Place ingredients in a blender and blend until smooth. Adjust ingredients to your own taste. Add more sugar if it is too tart and more or less ice or soda if it is too thin or thick.

2. Dip the rims of your glasses in lime juice and then into coarse salt or sugar. Pour mocktail into prepared glasses and garnish with additional strawberries.

INGREDIENTS:

2 Tbsp. seafood seasoning

3 garlic cloves, minced

⅓ cup lime juice

3 Tbsp. lemon juice

 2 lbs. raw shrimp, peeled and deveined

1 Tbsp. olive oil

flour tortillas, soft taco size

LIME CREMA:

1 cup sour cream

4 tsp. minced cilantro

1 Tbsp. lime juice

½ tsp. cumin

FOR SERVING: shredded cabbage, roasted corn, red pepper, mango, shredded cheese, or your favorite toppings

30-Minute Shrimp Tacos with Lime Crema

 pt 15 minutes   **ct** 10 minutes   **S** Serves 6

These shrimp tacos are super fast and easy to make—even with a quick marinade, you can have dinner on the table in about 30 minutes. And with a kicked-up lime cream drizzle, these fun shrimp tacos are a great way to jazz up your next taco night. Try adding mango as a garnish when it is in season.

INSTRUCTIONS:

1. Combine seasoning and garlic in a long, shallow dish. Add lime juice, lemon juice, and shrimp. Turn to coat. Cover and chill for 10 minutes.

2. Heat olive oil in a large pan over medium–high heat. Remove shrimp from marinade and add to the pan. Cook for 2–3 minutes on each side until pink and no longer opaque.

3. Spoon into warm tortillas and add cheese, shredded cabbage, roasted corn, and red pepper.

4. Mix together all ingredients for lime crema. Drizzle all over tacos and serve.

INGREDIENTS:

3 Tbsp. butter or coconut oil

3 tsp. minced garlic

2 cups jasmine rice

1 (13.5-oz.) can light coconut milk

2 cups water

splash white vinegar

juice and zest of one lime

salt and pepper

Coconut-Lime Rice

 pt 5 minutes   **ct** 20 minutes   **s** Serves 8

Made with fragrant Jasmine rice and coconut milk, you'll find that rice doesn't have to be a boring side dish any more!

INSTRUCTIONS:

1. Melt butter (or coconut oil) in a medium saucepan over medium heat. Add garlic and sauté until tender. Add rice and stir until coated with butter.

2. Add coconut milk and water. Bring to a boil. Reduce heat, cover, and simmer for 15–20 minutes or until liquid is absorbed and the rice is tender.

3. Remove the lid, fluff with a fork, and add white vinegar, lime juice, and lime zest. Season with salt and pepper to taste.

INGREDIENTS:

5-6 cups broccoli crowns, cut into florets

3 Tbsp. olive oil

4 garlic cloves, minced

kosher salt and black pepper

crushed red pepper flakes

Garlicky Roasted Broccoli

 5 minutes   10-12 minutes   Serves 4-6

Think you don't like broccoli? Then you need to give this roasted version a try! It takes only a few minutes to prep—and the sprinkling of crushed red pepper flakes gives it just the perfect pop of flavor.

INSTRUCTIONS:

1. Preheat oven to 450°F. Line a baking sheet with foil and lightly spray with nonstick cooking spray.

2. Toss broccoli with olive oil and minced garlic in a large bowl to coat. Transfer to baking sheet and sprinkle with salt, pepper, and red pepper flakes to taste.

3. Roast until broccoli begins to brown, 10–12 minutes. Serve immediately.

INGREDIENTS:

2 tsp. garlic powder

2 tsp. chili powder

1 tsp. cumin

½ tsp. coriander

1 tsp. seasoned salt

1 lb. chicken breasts or thighs

2 Tbsp. vegetable oil

½ cup honey

2 tsp. (or more, to taste) Sriracha sauce

Sweet Heat-Grilled Chicken

 10 minutes 10 minutes Serves 4-6

The great thing about this chicken is that you can make it as spicy as you'd like—it's actually fairly sweet. If you want to bump up the heat, you can add some cayenne, chipotle powder, or some additional Sriracha. If you haven't heard of Sriracha, it's an Asian chili sauce that you can find in the international food aisle of your grocery store (look for the bottle with a rooster on it). We love grilling this outside during the summer, but we make it just as often during the winter months using an indoor grill pan.

INSTRUCTIONS:

1. Preheat grill to medium high heat.

2. Prepare rub by combining the garlic powder, chili powder, cumin, coriander, and seasoned salt in a small bowl. Trim the fat from the chicken. Rinse and pat dry with a paper towel. Drizzle the chicken with vegetable oil, and press the rub firmly into both sides of the chicken. Grill for about 5 minutes on each side or until cooked through.

3. While the chicken is cooking, combine the honey and the Sriracha in a small bowl, stirring well. Brush glaze on the chicken during the final moments of cooking.

INGREDIENTS:

16 oz. small shelled pasta

1 cup mayonnaise

½ tsp. dried chives

¾ tsp. dried parsley

¼ tsp. dill weed

¼ tsp. garlic powder

¼ tsp. onion powder

¼ tsp. salt

¼ tsp. pepper

½ cup milk

4-6 slices bacon, cooked and crumbled

1½ cups grape tomatoes, halved

1 cup broccoli florets

⅓ cup sliced olives

Bacon Ranch Pasta Salad

 10 minutes   15 minutes   Serves 8

This creamy pasta salad is perfect for barbecues and cookouts—and you can easily change up the vegetable add-ins depending on your preferences. Making your own ranch dressing is really a snap and takes no time at all!

INSTRUCTIONS:

1. Cook pasta according to package directions; drain.

2. For ranch dressing, combine mayonnaise, chives, parsley, dill weed, garlic powder, onion powder, salt, and pepper in a large bowl. Whisk in milk until smooth.

3. Stir in pasta, bacon, and vegetables. Toss to coat. Cover and chill at least 1 hour in the refrigerator before serving. Toss with additional milk if needed.

INGREDIENTS:

½ cup vanilla yogurt

1 Tbsp. honey

2 tsp. lime juice

½ tsp. vanilla

½ tsp. poppy seeds

Vanilla Yogurt Poppy Seed Dip with Fresh Fruit

 15 minutes   n/a   Serves 4-6

People are more likely to eat anything if they can dip it! This is a great, healthy way to get kids (and adults!) to eat their fruit. Plus it makes a fun presentation. If you're entertaining, try serving the fruit on skewers.

INSTRUCTIONS:

1. Combine all ingredients in a medium bowl. Keep refrigerated until serving.

2. Serve with your favorite fresh fruit—we like strawberries, cantaloupe, pineapple, and grapes.

INGREDIENTS:

1 lb. boneless chicken (breasts or thighs)

2-3 limes, juiced

2 Tbsp. red wine vinegar

4 garlic cloves, minced

1 Tbsp. olive oil or butter

2 Tbsp. homemade taco seasoning

HOMEMADE TACO SEASONING:

4 Tbsp. chili powder

1 tsp. garlic powder

1 tsp. onion powder

1 tsp. crushed red pepper flakes (or more, to taste)

¼ tsp. cayenne

2 tsp. paprika

2 Tbsp. cumin

3 tsp. smoked sea salt (regular sea salt works fine too)

4 tsp. fresh black pepper

Fiesta-Lime Chicken

 4-8 hours   20 minutes   Serves 4

Jazz up your weeknights with this quick and easy Fiesta-Lime Chicken. Eat it plain, with beans or rice, or use it as a base for any Mexican-inspired meal!

INSTRUCTIONS:

1. Place chicken in a large resealable bag or a container with a lid. Squeeze the juice of the limes over the chicken, and add minced garlic and red wine vinegar. Toss to coat and refrigerate 4–8 hours.

2. When you are ready to cook your chicken, melt 1 tablespoon butter or olive oil in a heavy bottomed pan over medium–high heat. Rub taco seasoning over chicken pieces and place the chicken in the pan. Cook the chicken until browned, 7–10 minutes. Remove chicken and shred.

TACO SEASONING:

Making your own taco seasoning doesn't take much more time to make than tearing open one of those single–serving packets, and tastes oodles better. Just add all ingredients to an airtight container and shake to combine. Use approximately 2 tablespoons for each pound of meat—but adjust to fit your own tastes. This recipe makes about ⅔ cup, and will keep for about 6 months in an airtight container stored at room temperature.

INGREDIENTS:

⅔ cup flour

½ cup yellow cornmeal

3 Tbsp. sugar

1 Tbsp. baking powder

¼ tsp. salt

1 (15-oz.) can whole kernel corn, drained

1 (15-oz.) can cream corn, undrained

1 cup sour cream

½ cup (8 Tbsp.) unsalted butter, melted

Easy Creamy Corn Casserole

 pt 15 minutes   **ct** 50 minutes   **s** Serves 6-8

This savory side dish complements any meal and is so simple to throw together—even on a weeknight!

INSTRUCTIONS:

1. Preheat oven to 350°F. Spray an 8 × 8 casserole dish or a 9–inch deep pie plate with nonstick cooking spray.

2. Combine flour, cornmeal, sugar, baking powder, and salt in a large bowl. Stir well.

3. Add remaining ingredients to the flour mixture, stirring together with a rubber spatula. Pour mixture into greased casserole dish or pie plate.

4. Bake for 50 minutes, uncovered, or until golden brown. Serve immediately.

INGREDIENTS:

1½ cups red grapes

1½ cups green grapes

2 cups blueberries

2 cups strawberries, hulled and sliced

1 (6-oz.) container raspberries

1 (8-oz.) can pineapple chunks, drained, with juice reserved

5 oz. (half of a 10-oz. can) non-alcoholic piña colada drink mix, thawed

1/8 tsp. coconut extract

1/8 tsp. almond extract

FOR SERVING:
shredded coconut

Pineapple-Coconut Fruit Salad

 5 minutes   ct n/a   s Serves 6-8

This fun spin on fruit salad is a perfect side dish for spring or summer. Other fruits would work great in this salad as well, such as mango, papaya, or kiwi. Try adding in sliced bananas just before serving!

INSTRUCTIONS:

1. Combine fruit in a large serving bowl.

2. In a small bowl, whisk together thawed drink mix, reserved pineapple juice, and coconut and almond extracts. Pour mixture over fruit and toss to coat. Refrigerate until ready to serve.

3. Serve sprinkled with shredded coconut, if desired.

INGREDIENTS:

1 lb. chicken breasts, cut into bite-sized pieces

salt and pepper

1 cup cornstarch

2 eggs

¼ cup canola oil

SAUCE:

¾ cup sugar

4 Tbsp. ketchup

½ cup apple cider vinegar

1 Tbsp. soy sauce

1 tsp. garlic salt

1 cup bell pepper, cut into large chunks (any color, or a combination)

1 cup pineapple, cut into chunks (may use 20-oz. can, drained)

FOR SERVING: chopped green onion and sesame seeds

Sweet and Sour Chicken

 25 minutes   60 minutes   Serves 4-6

Skip the take-out and make your own sweet and sour chicken at home. While this recipe does take some hands-on prep time, you can feel good about feeding this meal to your family, especially since it's baked—not fried. Try adding in different vegetables depending on your family's preferences.

INSTRUCTIONS:

1. Preheat oven to 325°F.

2. Sprinkle chicken pieces with salt and pepper. Place 1 cup cornstarch in resealable bag and toss chicken in bag. Shake to coat, making sure bag is sealed first.

3. Whisk egg in a pie plate or shallow bowl. Remove chicken from bag and dip in eggs to coat.

4. Heat oil in a heavy bottomed skillet over medium heat. Cook chicken until browned but not cooked all the way through. Place chicken in a 9 × 13 baking dish.

5. In a medium bowl, whisk together sugar, ketchup, vinegar, soy sauce, and garlic salt. Stir in bell pepper and pineapple chunks, and pour sauce over chicken. Bake for 1 hour, turning the chicken every 15 minutes to coat. Serve with fried rice.

INGREDIENTS:

2 Tbsp. sesame oil

¼ cup chopped onion (red or yellow)

¼ cup chopped carrots

½ cup sliced mushrooms

2 garlic cloves, minced

2 cups shredded cabbage

3 cups cooked white rice, cooled

3 Tbsp. soy sauce (low-sodium)

½ tsp. garlic powder

½ tsp. onion powder

¼ tsp. celery salt

salt and pepper

Fried Rice

 pt 15 minutes   **ct** 20 minutes   **s** Serves 4–6

This easy fried rice is the perfect complement to any Asian-inspired meal. Make sure to used leftover, chilled rice. Hot or even warm rice will turn out mushy. You can easily turn this side dish into a main course by adding in protein such as chicken, shrimp, or scrambled eggs.

INSTRUCTIONS:

1. Heat sesame oil in a large skillet over medium heat. Add onion, carrots, mushrooms, garlic, and cabbage, and sauté until the vegetables are tender.

2. Add the cooked rice, soy sauce, garlic powder, onion powder, and celery salt and warm through. Add salt and pepper to taste.

Quick Pineapple Pie

 15 minutes   1 hour chill time   Serves 8

Pies don't have to be labor intensive to be both tasty and impressive. This easy and crowd-pleasing recipe came straight out of my grandmother's recipe box and is sure to be a winner for any occasion.

INGREDIENTS:

1 prepared graham cracker crust (found in baking aisle)

1 (14-oz.) can sweetened condensed milk

¼ cup lemon juice

1 (20-oz.) can crushed pineapple, drained

1 (8-oz.) container whipped topping, thawed

½ cup chopped pecans (optional)

maraschino cherries

INSTRUCTIONS:

1. Pour the can of sweetened condensed milk into a large bowl and whisk by hand until creamy. Add in lemon juice, pineapple chunks, whipped topping, and pecans (if using). Stir to combine.

2. Carefully spoon filling mixture into graham cracker crust. Chill at least one hour until ready to serve. Garnish with cherries, if desired.

Cream of Mushroom Soup

INGREDIENTS:

⅔ cup chicken stock

⅓ cup milk

3 Tbsp. flour

¼ cup finely diced fresh mushrooms

¼ tsp. salt

⅛ tsp. garlic powder

⅛ tsp. pepper

⅛ tsp. onion powder

INSTRUCTIONS:

1. Bring chicken stock to a boil in a small saucepan over medium–high heat.

2. In a small bowl, whisk together milk and flour until flour is dissolved. Slowly pour the milk–flour mixture into the boiling chicken stock, whisking to combine. Add the mushrooms and spices, and reduce the heat to medium. Bring the mixture back to a low boil and keep it there for about 3 minutes or until thickened.

3. Remove pan from heat until ready to use in step 4 in World's Best Chicken Pie instructions.

World's Best Chicken Pie

 30 minutes   60 minutes   Serves 6

I made this dish for my husband on our first wedding anniversary (and every year since), and I think he fell in love with me all over again. Don't be put off by the long ingredient list—while this recipe is labor intensive, it isn't difficult, and it is well worth the effort.

INGREDIENTS:

1 (14.1-oz.) package refrigerated pie crusts

2 Tbsp. butter

1 lb. chicken breasts, diced into small chunks

1 medium yellow onion, diced

½ cup sliced mushrooms

⅓ cup sliced carrots

1 celery stalk, sliced

⅓ cup white cooking wine

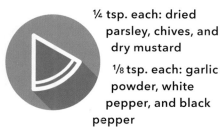 ¼ tsp. each: dried parsley, chives, and dry mustard

⅛ tsp. each: garlic powder, white pepper, and black pepper

1 Tbsp. Worcestershire sauce

1 cup chicken stock

1 bay leaf

1 Tbsp. cornstarch

1 recipe Cream of Mushroom / Soup (see page 36)

½ cup sour cream

½ cup shredded swiss cheese

½ cup shredded cheddar cheese

2 Tbsp. grated Parmesan cheese

INSTRUCTIONS:

1. Preheat oven to 400°F. Place 1 pie crust in a lightly greased 9–inch deep pie plate.

2. Melt butter in a large skillet over medium heat, and add diced chicken and onions. Sauté until onions are translucent and chicken is cooked through. Add mushrooms, carrots, and remaining ingredients through the bay leaf. Cover and allow the mixture to simmer for 10 minutes. Meanwhile, prepare your Cream of Mushroom Soup (see page 36).

3. After the chicken mixture has simmered, remove the lid and remove the bay leaf. In a small bowl, combine cornstarch with 2 tablespoons water. Stir the cornstarch mixture into the chicken and vegetable mixture, and bring to a boil, stirring occasionally.

4. Remove skillet from heat, and stir in Cream of Mushroom Soup, sour cream, and cheeses. Spoon mixture over pie crust, and top with remaining pie crust. Cut 4 to 5 slits in the top of the pie for steam to escape.

5. Bake for 40–50 minutes or until golden brown and bubbly.

INGREDIENTS:

3 lbs. potatoes, peeled and very thinly sliced

8 oz. cream cheese

1 cup milk

salt and pepper, to taste

4 garlic cloves, minced

²⁄₃ cup fresh Parmesan cheese, shredded and separated

¹⁄₃ cup cheddar cheese (optional)

Creamy Cheesy Scalloped Potatoes

 15 minutes   75 minutes   Serves 6

This is how my mom makes her scalloped potatoes—so easy, cheesy, and always crowd pleasing. The great thing about this classic comfort food is that it goes with everything from World's Best Chicken Pie (page 37) to Honey Mustard Pork Tenderloin (page 61). Just make sure to slice your potatoes thinly and uniformly.

INSTRUCTIONS:

1. Preheat oven to 350°F.

2. Soften cream cheese in microwave for 20–30 seconds until you can easily whisk it by hand. Whisk in milk, salt and pepper, and garlic until well blended.

3. Layer half of the potatoes in bottom of an 8 × 8 baking dish and pour half of the cream cheese mixture over the top. Sprinkle with ¹⁄₃ cup Parmesan cheese. Top with half of cheddar cheese, if using. Repeat layers and cover with aluminum foil.

4. Bake for 75 minutes (uncovering after 45 minutes), or until potatoes are tender and the sauce is hot and bubbly.

INGREDIENTS:

1 cup flour

1½ tsp. baking powder

½ tsp. salt

½ cup milk

¼ cup mayonnaise

Simple No-Roll Biscuits

 pt 5 minutes   ct 10 minutes   s Serves 8

My grandmother used to make these biscuits often—they really are simple! Since you just drop the batter into muffin tins, there is no rolling—or cutting—of the biscuits involved. These little biscuits bake up super moist and tender, and the mayonnaise doesn't affect the taste at all. If you keep self-rising flour in your pantry, you can use it in place of flour, baking powder, and salt.

INSTRUCTIONS:

1. Preheat oven to 400°F.

2. Whisk together flour, baking powder, and salt in a medium bowl. Stir in milk and mayonnaise until smooth, and divide the mixture evenly between 8 greased muffin cups. Bake for 10 minutes, or until the tops are lightly golden.

INGREDIENTS:

2 eggs

1½ cups Panko crumbs

6 Tbsp. Parmesan cheese, divided

1 tsp. dried basil

½ tsp. dried thyme

1 Tbsp. dried oregano

½ tsp. garlic powder

6 skinless, boneless chicken breasts, pounded thin

1 cup mozzarella cheese

16 oz. spaghetti noodles, cooked according to package directions (optional)

SAUCE:

1 (28-oz.) jar crushed tomatoes

2 Tbsp. dried parsley

2 Tbsp. dried basil

3 garlic cloves, minced

red pepper flakes, to taste

Baked Chicken Parmesan

 20 minutes   55 minutes   Serves 6

This chicken Parmesan is easy enough to throw together on a weeknight, but tasty enough to serve for company. And, because it's baked and not fried, you don't have to feel quite so guilty about eating it. If you're not familiar with Panko crumbs, it is a Japanese-style breadcrumb made from crustless bread. Panko generally stays crispier longer than regular breadcrumbs because they don't absorb as much liquid—that's why I prefer using them over regular breadcrumbs in this recipe.

INSTRUCTIONS:

1. Preheat oven to 350°F. Spray a 9 × 13 baking dish with nonstick cooking spray.

2. Whisk eggs in a shallow dish or pie plate. In a second dish or pie plate, combine Panko, two tablespoons Parmesan, basil, thyme, oregano, and garlic powder. Dip each chicken piece in the eggs and then coat with Panko mixture, pressing the Panko into the chicken. Repeat, dipping the chicken into the egg and into the Panko for a second coating.

3. Place the chicken into the prepared baking dish and bake for 40 minutes.

4. While chicken is baking, prepare sauce by combining all sauce ingredients into a medium bowl. Pour sauce over chicken and top with 1 cup mozzarella cheese and 4 tablespoons Parmesan cheese. Continue baking until chicken is no longer pink in the center and the cheese has melted, approximately 15 more minutes.

5. Serve chicken with cooked spaghetti noodles, if desired.

DRESSING:

¾ cup mayonnaise or Greek yogurt

2 Tbsp. apple cider vinegar

2 Tbsp. sugar

½ tsp. salt

½ tsp. pepper

INGREDIENTS:

3½ cups broccoli, cut into bite-sized pieces

¼ cup diced red onion

8 oz. cheddar cheese, cubed

½ cup grape tomatoes, halved

½ cup raisins or dried cranberries

4 slices bacon, cooked and crumbled

½ cup toasted pecans (optional)

Creamy Broccoli Salad

 15 minutes   n/a   Serves 4–6

I first tried this recipe years ago at a work function. Even though it uses mayonnaise (which I don't usually love), I gobbled up this salad like crazy and knew I had to have the recipe. This is a perfect dish for entertaining, because it's just as great at room temperature as it is cold. If using bacon and nuts, make sure to sprinkle those on right before serving so they don't get soggy.

INSTRUCTIONS:

1. In a small bowl, combine mayonnaise, vinegar, sugar, salt, and pepper. Whisk until smooth and set aside.

2. In a large bowl, combine broccoli, onion, cheese, tomatoes, and raisins. Add the dressing and toss to coat. Cover and refrigerate until ready to serve.

3. Just before serving, toss cooked bacon and toasted pecans (optional) over the salad. Taste and adjust seasonings if necessary. Serve cold or at room temperature.

INGREDIENTS:

2 (4-oz.) white chocolate bars, roughly chopped

1 cup heavy whipping cream

FOR SERVING: raspberries

Two-Ingredient White Chocolate Mousse

 20 minutes n/a Serves 4

Who says dessert has to be time-consuming or contain a long list of ingredients? This light-as-a-cloud white chocolate mousse takes only two ingredients—and only about 10 (active) minutes of your time. But served with fresh raspberries (or any other fresh fruit of your choosing), no one will ever guess how little effort this dessert actually entailed.

INSTRUCTIONS:

1. Combine chopped white chocolate and cream in a large microwave–safe bowl. Microwave at half power for 3–3½ minutes but do not allow the mixture to boil. Whisk to combine, making sure the mixture is smooth and shiny.

2. Set microwave–safe bowl down into a bowl of ice water and let stand until completely cool, 10–15 minutes, stirring often. Remove from ice and beat with an electric mixture until soft peaks form.

3. Cover and refrigerate until ready to serve.

4. Spoon into bowls and top with fresh raspberries when serving, if desired.

INGREDIENTS:

1 (8-oz.) container sour cream

1 garlic clove, minced

½ tsp. chili powder

½ tsp. ground cumin

¼ tsp. kosher salt

2 Tbsp. chopped fresh cilantro

1 Tbsp. fresh lime juice

½ cup Mexican blend shredded cheese

2 cups shredded, cooked chicken

8 flour tortillas, soft taco size

Baked Creamy Chicken Chimichangas

 10 minutes   15 minutes   Serves 8

If you like restaurant-style chimichangas but don't like the calories that come along with them, try making this baked version at home. By giving them a light spray of olive oil and a sprinkling of kosher salt, they'll crisp up nicely in the oven and you'll never miss all the grease or calories!

INSTRUCTIONS:

1. Preheat oven to 350°F.

2. Whisk together sour cream, garlic, chili powder, cumin, and salt. Whisk in cilantro and lime juice until smooth. Add in cheese and chicken to combine.

3. Fill each tortilla with approximately ¼ cup chicken mixture. Roll up and secure with a toothpick. Spray each tortilla with olive oil and sprinkle with kosher salt.

4. Place tortillas on a large baking sheet and bake for 15–20 minutes until tortillas are lightly golden brown, turning once halfway through.

INGREDIENTS:

2 Tbsp. olive oil

4 garlic cloves, minced

2 tsp. cumin

1 tsp. chili powder

1 tsp. coriander

1½ tsp. oregano

1 tsp. salt

½ tsp. pepper

2 (15-oz.) cans pinto beans, undrained

½ lime, juiced

Stove Top Refried Beans

 pt 5 minutes   ct 10 minutes   s Serves 4

Authentic refried beans typically involve a long soaking process, a long cooking process, and bacon grease—all things I don't want to mess with, especially on a work night. But while we do love refried beans, we also don't love the congealed mess that comes out of the prepared cans you can purchase at the grocery store. This quick stovetop version is a great compromise your family is sure to enjoy.

INSTRUCTIONS:

1. Heat olive oil in a large skillet over medium heat. Add garlic, cumin, chili powder, coriander, oregano, salt, and pepper. Sauté until fragrant—about 30 seconds.

2. Stir in both cans of undrained beans and cook, stirring occasionally, until beans are warmed through. Smash beans with a potato masher, or pulse with a food processor or blender. Squeeze lime juice over smashed beans, and stir to combine before serving.

Espinaca Casserole

 20 minutes   5 minutes   Serves 4-6

One of my favorite side dishes when eating Mexican food out is Espinaca—and now I've discovered how to make it at home. It's super simple to make, comes together in just a few minutes, and is just as good on its own served with chips or wrapped up inside a warm flour tortilla.

INGREDIENTS:

2 slices bacon

8 oz. fresh mushrooms, coarsely chopped

1 chipotle pepper in adobo sauce, finely chopped

½ cup diced red onion

¼ cup chopped red bell pepper

1 tsp. minced garlic

1½ tsp. seasoning salt

5 oz. white American cheese, cubed

3 oz. cream cheese, cubed

10 oz. frozen chopped spinach, thawed

1 cup frozen corn, thawed

½ cup shredded Mexican blend cheese

INSTRUCTIONS:

1. Preheat oven to 350°F. Sauté bacon in a medium skillet until crispy. Remove bacon from skillet and drain all but a small amount of grease. Add mushrooms, chipotle pepper, onion, red bell pepper, garlic, and seasoning salt. Sauté until the mushrooms and the onion are tender.

2. Keeping skillet on low heat, add white American cheese and cream cheese, and cook until cheese has melted, stirring constantly. Dice bacon.

3. Add spinach, corn, and bacon, and stir well. Cook for an additional 3 minutes. Pour mixture into a 1½–quart baking dish. Sprinkle shredded cheese on top and heat in oven until cheese has melted, about 5 minutes.

INGREDIENTS:

1 lb. lean ground beef

1 cup diced red onion

2 tsp. minced garlic

⅓ cup ketchup

5 Tbsp. yellow mustard

5 Tbsp. brown sugar

½ cup water

1 Tbsp. Worcestershire sauce

¼ tsp. red pepper flakes

salt and pepper, to taste

FOR SERVING: hamburger buns, sliced red onion, shredded pepper jack cheese, and Fritos

Sweet and Spicy Sloppy Joes

 pt 10 minutes   **ct** 20 minutes   **s** Serves 4

Sloppy Joes are a staple family-friendly dinner, at least at my house. But if you're looking to jazz up your old standby, give this sweet and spicy recipe a try. Piled high with shredded pepper jack cheese and Fritos, these sandwiches are not the boring version you grew up with! You can easily control the heat in these sandwiches by adding more red pepper flakes, if desired.

INSTRUCTIONS:

1. Brown ground beef over medium heat in a large skillet. Add in diced onion and minced garlic, and continue cooking until onion has softened, about 5 minutes.

2. Stir in remaining ingredients and bring the mixture to a boil. Reduce heat and simmer for at least 20 minutes (the longer the better), or until the mixture thickens slightly.

3. Serve on your favorite bun or roll and top with red onion slices, shredded pepper jack cheese, and Fritos.

INGREDIENTS:

4 medium russet potatoes, washed and cut into 8 wedges each (leave the skins on)

½ tsp. black pepper

2¼ tsp. garlic salt

¼ tsp. dried parsley

2 Tbsp. cornstarch

2 Tbsp. olive oil

DIPPING SAUCE:
⅔ cup ketchup

⅓ cup mayonnaise

½ tsp. dill pickle juice

½ tsp. seasoned salt

Crispy Oven-Baked Fries with Dipping Sauce

 10 minutes   45 minutes   Serves 4

Who needs burger joint fries when you can make your own at home? I use two tricks to get crispy fries in the oven. Soaking your pre-cut fries in water first causes some of the starches to leech out into the water (starch left in your potatoes keeps moisture from escaping, which leaves more water in the potato and leads to soggy fries). Adding a bit of cornstarch to your seasoning mixture also helps the fries crisp up. With a side of homemade dipping sauce, these fries are every bit as good as those from any diner!

INSTRUCTIONS:

1. Preheat oven to 400°F and line a large baking sheet with foil. Spray foil with cooking spray.

2. Cut potatoes (skins on) lengthwise into ⅓–inch fries. Place them in a large bowl of water and allow to sit for a few minutes. Drain and repeat. Rinse fries and pat them completely dry.

3. Mix spices, cornstarch, and oil in a medium bowl. Add fries and toss to coat. Place fries in a single layer on your prepared baking sheet, being careful not to crowd them. If they overlap, your fries will steam and will not get crispy.

4. Bake 40–45 minutes, turning once halfway through.

5. For your dipping sauce, stir together all ingredients. Makes 1 cup of sauce. Keep refrigerated up to 1 week.

INGREDIENTS:

1 pint (two cups) heavy whipping cream, very cold

1 can (14 ounces) sweetened condensed milk

2 oz. cream cheese, softened

2 Tbsp. butter, melted

1 cup finely chopped strawberries

FOR SERVING:
crushed graham crackers

No-Churn Strawberry Cheesecake Ice Cream

 10 minutes   6 hours   Serves 6

One of the best tricks I ever learned was how to make two-ingredient ice cream (no ice cream maker required!). With just whipping cream and sweetened condensed milk, you can have homemade ice cream any time you want, and with very little work! There are endless flavor combinations you can create, but this strawberry cheesecake version is always a favorite.

INSTRUCTIONS:

1. In a large bowl using a handheld mixer or a stand mixer fitted with the whisk attachment, whisk the heavy cream until stiff peaks form, 1–2 minutes.

2. In a second large bowl, whisk together sweetened condensed milk, cream cheese, and butter. With a rubber spatula, carefully fold strawberries and whipped cream into cream cheese mixture.

3. Pour the ice cream into a large container (about 2 quarts) and cover. Freeze until firm, about 6 hours.

INGREDIENTS:

½ cup low-sodium soy sauce

⅓ cup vegetable oil

3 Tbsp. whole grain garlic mustard

2 Tbsp. chopped fresh sage

4 tsp. honey

4 garlic cloves, minced

1½ tsp. ground black pepper

1 tsp. cider vinegar

1 lb. pork tenderloin

Honey-Mustard Pork Tenderloin

  pt 1 hour (mostly refrigeration time)   **ct** 50 minutes   **s** Serves 4-6

If you think pork is boring and flavorless—think again. This quick and easy marinade comes together with ingredients you probably already have in your kitchen and packs a flavor punch with the combination of soy, mustard, sage, and honey.

INSTRUCTIONS:

1. Combine soy sauce, vegetable oil, mustard, sage, honey, garlic, and black pepper in a small bowl. Separate ¼ cup of the marinade and stir the vinegar into it. Set aside.

2. Place the remaining marinade in a resealable bag and add the tenderloin. Seal tightly, pressing out all of the air. Refrigerate for 1 hour, turning the bag after 30 minutes to evenly marinate.

3. Remove pork from bag and allow the excess marinade to drip back into the bag. Discard bag and place tenderloin on a foil-lined baking sheet.

4. Bake at 350°F for 40–50 minutes, or until the pork is cooked through.

5. Remove from oven and brush with the reserved marinade. Tent loosely with foil for 10 minutes.

6. Slice and serve, adding any leftover marinade, if desired.

INGREDIENTS:

3 lbs. red potatoes, unpeeled, scrubbed and cubed

1 Tbsp. plus 2 tsp. kosher salt, divided

4 garlic cloves, minced

4 Tbsp. butter

1 cup half and half

½ cup sour cream

6 oz. Feta cheese

½ tsp. pepper

½ tsp. dried oregano

½ tsp. dried basil

Creamy Mashed Potatoes

 10 minutes   25 minutes   **s** Serves 6-8

Let's get real: with butter, half-and-half, and sour cream, there's nothing remotely healthy about this dish! But the next time you need mashed potatoes for a special meal, give this recipe a try—you won't be sorry. The addition of Feta cheese makes them extra creamy.

INSTRUCTIONS:

1. Place potatoes in a large saucepan. Cover with water and 1 tablespoon kosher salt. Bring to a boil; reduce heat and allow potatoes to cook 15–20 minutes, until tender. Drain and transfer to a large mixing bowl.

2. In a small saucepan, sauté the garlic in the butter for approximately 30 seconds, being careful not to burn. Add half–and–half to heat through.

3. Mix the potatoes with the paddle attachment of an electric mixer, just enough to break them up. Slowly add the cream mixture on low speed. Fold in the sour cream, feta cheese, remaining 2 teaspoons salt, pepper, oregano, and basil with a large rubber spatula. Serve immediately.

INGREDIENTS:

1 lb. fresh asparagus

½ tsp. kosher salt

¼ tsp. black pepper

1 Tbsp. olive oil

1 Tbsp. lemon juice (about half of a large lemon)

1 tsp. minced garlic

1-2 Tbsp. grated Parmesan cheese

Lemon-Parmesan Asparagus

 5 minutes   10 minutes   Serves 4

Drizzled with a mixture of olive oil, lemon juice, and garlic, this asparagus roasts just perfectly to fork tender. This recipe is a great way to get your family to eat vegetables—everything is better sprinkled with cheese, right? Even better, it requires very little work and hardly any oven time.

INSTRUCTIONS:

1. Preheat oven to 425°F.

2. Wash asparagus and snap off the woody ends, 2–3 inches off the bottoms.

3. Combine remaining ingredients except cheese in a large bowl. Add asparagus and toss to coat.

4. Line a baking sheet with foil and spray with nonstick cooking spray. Arrange the asparagus in a single layer on the baking sheet.

5. Roast for 10 minutes, turning once halfway through. Sprinkle with cheese just before serving.

INGREDIENTS:

2 Tbsp. olive oil

1 small red onion, diced

1-2 chipotle peppers in adobo, seeded and diced

2 tsp. minced garlic

2 lbs. lean ground beef

2 tsp. cornstarch

¼ cup lime juice

2 Tbsp. tomato paste

4 tsp. homemade taco seasoning (see page 25)

1 (15-oz.) can black beans, drained and rinsed

1 (14-oz.) can low-sodium beef broth

FOR SERVING: taco shells, shredded cheese, sour cream, chopped cilantro, pico de gallo, jalapeños

Beef and Bean Chipotle Tacos

 15 minutes   45 minutes   **s** Serves 4-6

Taco Tuesday is a real thing around our house—always a favorite because you can customize your own with toppings galore. This ground beef taco filling uses my favorite homemade taco seasoning, and the rest of the ingredients you most likely already have on hand. If you prefer, ground chicken or ground turkey works just as well in this recipe.

INSTRUCTIONS:

1. In a large skillet, sauté onion in olive oil over medium heat until tender, about 3 minutes. Add chipotle peppers and garlic, and cook for another minute. Add ground beef and cook until browned; drain meat mixture and return to heat.

2. Stir cornstarch into lime juice and whisk to combine. Add the lime juice mixture to cooked beef along with remaining ingredients.

3. Reduce mixture to a simmer and cook 35–40 minutes, or until liquid has evaporated.

4. Fill taco shells with beef and toppings of choice.

INGREDIENTS:

3 Tbsp. vegetable oil

1 cup long grain rice, uncooked

1 tsp. minced garlic

½ tsp. kosher salt

½ tsp. cumin

½ tsp. coriander

½ tsp. oregano

1 (8-oz.) can tomato sauce

1 (14-oz.) can chicken broth

Mexican-Style Rice

 pt 5 minutes   ct 20-25 minutes   s Serves 4

Have you ever craved Mexican-style rice from your favorite restaurant? Well, here it is, only without the restaurant price tag, and with significantly better flavor!

INSTRUCTIONS:

1. Heat oil in a large saucepan over medium heat. Add rice and toss to coat, stirring until rice begins to brown.

2. Add in garlic, salt, cumin, coriander, and oregano. Stir for another 2–3 minutes, or until rice just begins to look golden.

3. Add the tomato sauce and chicken broth, and bring the mixture to a boil. Cover and allow rice to simmer 20–25 minutes, or until liquid evaporates. Remove pan from heat and fluff rice with a fork.

INGREDIENTS:

1 prepared graham cracker crust (found in baking aisle)

1 (14-oz.) can dulce de leche*

4 bananas, sliced

1½ cups whipping cream

2 Tbsp. confectioner's sugar

1 tsp. vanilla extract

Caramel-Banana Pie

 15 minutes   1 hour chill time   Serves 8

Dulce de leche is a combination of milk and sugar that has been slowly cooked, making a thick and creamy caramelized spread. You can find it ready made in your grocery store next to the canned milk. When you combine it with sliced bananas, whipped cream, and graham crackers, the result is just marvelous. The best part is that this pie only takes a few minutes to assemble.

INSTRUCTIONS:

1. Pour dulce de leche into a small microwave–safe bowl and heat 15–20 seconds, or until the sauce is smooth enough to spread easily. Pour half of dulce de leche over graham cracker crust. Top with half of the banana slices and pour remaining dulce de leche over the bananas. Top with remaining banana slices.

2. Beat whipping cream, confectioner's sugar, and vanilla extract until soft peaks form in a large mixing bowl with an electric mixer. Spoon cream over bananas, and garnish with additional sliced bananas, if desired. Chill 1 hour before serving.

* DULCE DE LECHE:

Did you know you can make your own dulce de leche? It's easy! You'll start with a 14–oz. can of sweetened condensed milk. Remove the label from the can and pierce three holes in the formation of a triangle on top of the can. This is important—the holes allow pressure to release from the can so it does not explode. Place the can in a saucepan, and fill the pan with water three–quarters of the way up the sides of the can.

Bring the water to a simmer for 3–4 hours, adding more water as necessary. Use tongs to remove the can from the water. Cool slightly.

INGREDIENTS:

1 Tbsp. olive oil

3 garlic cloves, minced

3 Tbsp. chili powder

1 Tbsp. cumin

1 Tbsp. onion powder

1 tsp. salt

¼ tsp. oregano

1 (15-oz.) can tomato sauce

1 cup chicken stock

Homemade Enchilada Sauce

 5 minutes   10 minutes   Makes 2 cups

This easy homemade enchilada sauce takes just a few minutes to make and tastes worlds better than anything you can buy on your grocer's shelf.

INSTRUCTIONS:

1. Heat oil in a medium saucepan over medium–high heat. Stir in garlic, chili powder, cumin, onion powder, salt, and oregano. Cook for about 30 seconds, stirring constantly. Sautéing your spices for a few seconds will give your sauce a fuller flavor.

2. Add in tomato sauce and chicken stock. Bring mixture to a simmer and cook 8–10 minutes, stirring occasionally.

3. Remove from heat. Use immediately in Beef and Cheese Enchiladas (page 74), or keep refrigerated for up to one week.

INGREDIENTS:

1½ lbs. lean ground beef

1 medium yellow onion, diced

1 (4-oz.) can diced green chilies

1 tsp. kosher salt

½ tsp. pepper

1 Tbsp. chili powder

1 tsp. cumin

½ tsp. coriander

½ tsp. oregano

1 batch homemade enchilada sauce (page 73), or 2 cups of your favorite sauce, divided

3 cups Mexican blend shredded cheese, divided

10 corn tortillas

FOR SERVING: sour cream, cilantro, green onion, olives

Beef and Cheese Enchiladas

 15 minutes   20-25 minutes   Serves 8-10

Loaded with crumbly beef and lots of cheesy goodness, these hearty beef and cheese enchiladas go from kitchen to table in no time!

INSTRUCTIONS:

1. Preheat oven to 350°F.

2. Cook beef and onion in a large skillet oven medium–high heat until onion is translucent and meat is fully cooked. Drain meat and return to heat.

3. Add green chilies, salt, pepper, and spices, and cook 1–2 minutes more. Remove from heat and stir in ½ cup enchilada sauce and 1 cup shredded cheese.

4. Pour about ¼ cup sauce into the bottom of on 9 × 13 pan. Place ¼ cup filling in each tortilla and roll up tightly, placing seam–side down in pan. Top with remaining sauce and 2 cups cheese.

5. Bake uncovered 20–25 minutes, or until cheese is melted and bubbly.

INGREDIENTS:

1 (15-oz.) can black beans, drained and rinsed

1 cup corn

½ red, green, and yellow bell peppers, diced

½ red onion, diced

1 jalapeño, seeded and diced

⅓ cup roughly chopped cilantro leaves

VINAIGRETTE:

6 Tbsp. red wine vinegar

¼ cup honey

juice of 1 lime

3 Tbsp. olive oil

3 garlic cloves, minced

salt and pepper, to taste

Tri-Color Pepper Salad with Honey-Lime Vinaigrette

 15 minutes   n/a   Serves 6

I've been making a version of this colorful pepper salad every year since my husband and I were married. You may change up the peppers in this recipe depending on what is in season and the prices of the peppers in your market, but this salad is especially great with a variety of colors.

INSTRUCTIONS:

1.   Combine black beans, corn, diced peppers, onion, jalapeño, and chopped cilantro in a large bowl.

2.   In a small bowl, whisk together vinaigrette ingredients. Pour dressing over vegetables. Cover and refrigerate for at least 1 hour before serving.

Chicken Lettuce Wraps

 15 minutes   10 minutes   Serves 6

Skip going out for lettuce wraps when you can make your own at home. Filled with chicken, bell pepper, and water chestnuts, these are both healthy and yummy. Fresh ginger and lots of garlic make these extra delicious, and you can kick the spice up a notch by adjusting the red pepper flakes to your family's preferences. You can find plum sauce in the international foods aisle at your grocery store.

INGREDIENTS:

2 Tbsp. olive oil

1 lb. boneless chicken breasts, finely chopped

2 Tbsp. minced fresh ginger

4 garlic cloves, minced

1 bell pepper, diced (any color)

1 (8-oz.) can water chestnuts, finely chopped

red pepper flakes, to taste

½ cup plum sauce (an 8-oz. jar)

1 Tbsp. soy sauce

6 iceberg lettuce leaves

FOR SERVING: rice noodles and shredded carrots

INSTRUCTIONS:

1. Heat a large skillet to high heat. Add olive oil and chicken. Cook chicken for 2 minutes, stirring occasionally. Add ginger, garlic, bell pepper, water chestnuts, and red pepper flakes. Cook for another 2 minutes, or until the chicken is cooked through.

2. Add plum sauce and soy sauce, and stir to combine.

3. Transfer mixture to a serving bowl. Spoon into lettuce leaves and top with shredded carrots and rice noodles, if desired.

INGREDIENTS:

½ cup soy sauce

¼ cup cider vinegar

¼ cup light brown sugar

1 Tbsp. cornstarch

2 tsp. finely chopped fresh ginger

2 garlic cloves, finely minced

¼ tsp. crushed red pepper flakes, to taste

1 lb. boneless pork loin, cut into ⅛–inch strips

2 tsp. olive oil, divided

1 red bell pepper, cut into strips

2 cups broccoli crowns, cut into florets

FOR SERVING: cooked rice, diced green onion, and sesame seeds

30-Minute Pork Stir Fry

pt 20 minutes   **ct** 10 minutes   **s** Serves 4

True story: one of our wedding gifts was a really nice, big wok . . . which we promptly caught on fire while making a stir fry one night. We've since learned how to keep the flames out of the kitchen, and this easy meal is one of our favorites. You can really use any combination of vegetables that your family likes—I like the brightness of the red peppers and the broccoli, but snap peas and carrots would work just as well.

INSTRUCTIONS:

1. Combine soy sauce, vinegar, brown sugar, and cornstarch in a large bowl and whisk to combine. Stir in ginger, garlic, and red pepper flakes. Add pork strips to marinade mixture and toss to coat. Cover and refrigerate for 15 minutes.

2. Heat 1 teaspoon oil in a large skillet over high heat. Remove pork from marinade and spoon into skillet, reserving marinade. Cook pork until no longer pink, about 2 minutes. Remove pork to a plate and tent with foil to keep warm.

3. Heat remaining 1 teaspoon oil in skillet, and add bell pepper and broccoli. Stir–fry vegetables until crisp tender, 2–3 minutes. Return pork to skillet and stir in reserved marinade. Bring mixture to a boil, and cook until the sauce is thickened.

4. Serve pork and vegetables over cooked rice and sprinkle with chopped green onions and sesame seeds, if desired.

INGREDIENTS:

1 (14-oz.) can sweetened condensed milk

¾ cup creamy peanut butter

2 cups baking mix (or Bisquick)

1 tsp. vanilla

¼ cup sugar

¼ cup sprinkles (optional)

1 (13-oz.) pkg. milk chocolate kisses

Peanut Butter Kissed Cookies

 10 minutes   11 minutes   Makes 36

There is a reason these simple peanut butter and chocolate cookies are in grandmothers' recipe boxes all over the country—they're a classic. They are quick, simple, and best of all: you simply can't beat the combination of peanut butter and chocolate. For a fun twist, change the color of the sprinkles to match the season or the holiday!

INSTRUCTIONS:

1. Preheat oven to 350°F. Line baking sheets with parchment paper or spray with nonstick cooking spray.

2. Using an electric mixer at medium speed, beat sweetened condensed milk and peanut butter until creamy. Reduce speed to low; add baking mix and vanilla and beat until just blended.

3. Put sugar into a separate bowl. Shape dough into 1–inch balls, and roll them in sugar. You may also roll them in sprinkles, if you want. Place on prepared baking sheets. Bake for 11 minutes, or until tops of cookies are lightly golden.

4. Remove from oven and immediately place an unwrapped chocolate kiss in the center, pressing down. Remove cookies to wire racks to cool.

INGREDIENTS:

1 lb. lean ground beef

1 medium red onion, diced

1 tsp. salt

¼ tsp. pepper

1 Tbsp. chili powder

 1 tsp. cumin

½ tsp. coriander

½ tsp. oregano

1 (4.5-oz.) can sliced black olives

1 (8-oz.) can tomato sauce

2 cups grated sharp cheddar cheese, divided

6 small corn tortillas (taco size)

⅔ cup water

Deep Dish Enchilada Pie

 15 minutes   30 minutes   s Serves 4–6

This was a staple dish in my home growing up, and even a picky eater like me gobbled it up. While the method of pouring water into your pie dish may sound odd—your tortillas will absorb the liquid during the baking process. Serve up your pie with all of your favorite Mexican toppings!

INSTRUCTIONS:

1. Preheat oven to 400°F.

2. Brown ground beef and onion together in a large skillet over medium heat until meat is no longer pink. Add salt, pepper, chili powder, cumin, coriander, oregano, olives, and tomato sauce. Continue to cook for a few more minutes.

3. In a 2–quart casserole dish or a deep–dish pie plate alternate layers of meat mixture and cheese between tortillas, starting and ending with the tortillas. Reserve at least ½ cup cheese. Pour ⅔ cup water over your layered pie. Top with remaining cheese.

4. Cover dish with aluminum foil and bake for 30 minutes.

INGREDIENTS:

2 Tbsp. olive oil

2 Tbsp. chopped garlic

1 medium red onion, finely chopped

1 large jalapeño pepper, finely chopped

1 tsp. oregano

1 tsp. cumin

1 tsp. coriander

2 (15-oz.) cans black beans, drained and rinsed

1 cup broth (beef, chicken or vegetable)

½ cup chopped fresh cilantro

2 Tbsp. fresh lime juice

Perfectly Seasoned Black Beans

 10 minutes   20-25 minutes   **S** Serves 6

Even if you think you don't care for black beans, give this recipe a try. The flavors marry together to turn boring black beans into a truly sensational side dish! Try mashing the beans a bit and serving with tortilla chips for an appetizer, or rolling them up in a tortilla with a bit of shredded pepper jack cheese for a quick and easy lunch.

INSTRUCTIONS:

1. Heat olive oil over medium heat in a medium saucepan. Add garlic, onion, and jalapeño to the warm oil. Add oregano, cumin, and coriander, and sauté just until the onion starts to look translucent.

2. Add the black beans and broth, and bring the mixture to a boil. Reduce the heat and simmer 20–25 minutes. Add chopped cilantro and lime juice, and stir. Serve immediately.

INGREDIENTS:

CINNAMON CHIPS:

2 Tbsp. sugar

¼ tsp. cinnamon

3 Tbsp. butter, melted

10 (6-inch) flour tortillas

SALSA:

4 cups of your favorite seasonal fruit (here I used a combination of mango, blackberry, strawberry, and kiwi)

1 Tbsp. brown sugar

3 Tbsp. raspberry jam

Seasonal Fruit Salsa with Cinnamon Chips

 10 minutes   10 minutes   Serves 6

Fruit salsa makes a great snack, side dish, or even a light dessert that both kids and adults will enjoy. Any combination of fruit will work great here—just use a combination of your favorites and whatever is in season.

INSTRUCTIONS:

1. Preheat oven to 350°F.

2. Combine sugar and cinnamon in a small bowl. Brush melted butter over tortillas, and sprinkle the sugar mixture over the top. Using a pizza cutter, slice each tortilla into 8 wedges. Place tortilla wedges onto ungreased baking sheet and bake 10–12 minutes.

3. While the chips are baking, dice fruit. Sprinkle fruit with brown sugar and stir in jam. Once chips are cool, serve immediately with fruit salsa.

INGREDIENTS:

2 Tbsp. olive oil

2½ lbs. beef roast

kosher salt and pepper

2 cups water

2 cans low-sodium beef broth

½ cup dried onion flakes

2 Tbsp. low-sodium beef bouillon granules

½ tsp. onion powder

½ tsp. parsley flakes

¼ tsp. celery seed

3 garlic cloves, minced

2 bay leaves

6-8 slices provolone cheese

6-8 hoagie rolls

Slow Cooker French Dip Sandwiches

 15 minutes   8-10 hours   Serves 6-8

We make these sandwiches nearly once a week in the fall and winter—they are so easy, crowd-pleasing, and hearty. Make sure to use low-sodium beef broth so your meat and dipping juices aren't too salty. The longer this meat cooks, the better. If you can, start your slow cooker on high for an hour or so, then turn it down to low and continue cooking for another 8 hours.

INSTRUCTIONS:

1. Heat oil over medium-high heat in a large skillet. Generously season meat on all sides with salt and pepper. When the skillet is hot, place roast in the pan and sear it on all sides. You're not cooking it all the way through; just cook it until sides are brown. This seals in the juices.

2. Meanwhile, place remaining ingredients except cheese and rolls in the bottom of your slow cooker. Placed the seared meat on top.

3. Cook 8–10 hours on low or 4–5 hours on high. The meat is done when it is easily shredded with a fork. Remove the bay leaves and discard.

4. Pile shredded meat on bottoms of hoagie buns. Top with a slice of provolone cheese, and broil open-faced until the bun is just toasted. Serve with juices for dipping.

INGREDIENTS:

3 lbs. red potatoes, halved (or quartered, if large)

2 Tbsp. olive oil*

1/3 cup grated parmesan cheese**

kosher salt and pepper, to taste

5 garlic cloves, minced

2 Tbsp. minced fresh rosemary

2 Tbsp. butter

Rosemary-Parmesan Roasted Potatoes

 10 minutes   25-30 minutes   Serves 6

Potatoes are far and away my husband's most requested side dish—but plain old baked potatoes can get boring. These potatoes are garlicky, cheesy, and roasted to buttery perfection, with just the right amount of fresh rosemary.

INSTRUCTIONS:

1. Preheat oven to 400°F.

2. Line a baking sheet with foil and coat with nonstick spray. Place potatoes in a single layer and coat them with oil. Sprinkle with cheese, salt, and pepper. Add garlic and rosemary, and toss to coat.

3. Bake 25–30 minutes, or until potatoes are golden and crisp. Add butter and stir. Bake for 1 additional minute. Serve immediately.

* My grocery store sells a rosemary olive oil, which is perfect for this recipe. Regular olive oil works just fine too.

** Either fresh Parmesan or grated Parmesan in a container will work in this recipe.

INGREDIENTS:

4 cups popped popcorn, unseasoned (about one 3.5-oz. bag)

4 Tbsp. unsalted butter

16 large marshmallows

¾ cup light brown sugar

salt

¼ cup creamy peanut butter

¾ tsp. sea salt (optional)

Peanut Butter Marshmallow Popcorn

 n/a   **ct** 5 minutes   **s** Makes 4 cups

This was the first recipe my mother-in-law gave me after I got married. My husband loves this popcorn, and he still gets excited when I make it! It's a fun movie night popcorn or anytime treat, and it doesn't take long to make . . . the hardest part is waiting for it to cool before digging in.

INSTRUCTIONS:

1. Place popcorn in a large bowl, removing any unpopped kernels. Set aside.

2. In a heavy-bottomed saucepan, melt together butter, marshmallows, brown sugar, and a pinch of salt. Stir constantly until the mixture is smooth and bubbling. Remove from heat and stir in peanut butter.

3. Pour peanut butter mixture over popcorn and stir to coat. Spread on a cookie sheet to cool. Sprinkle with sea salt, if desired.

INGREDIENTS:

1 (2-lb.) pork tenderloin

1 (12-oz.) can root beer

2 cups barbecue sauce (your favorite) or homemade (see below)

BARBECUE SAUCE:

2 (8-oz.) cans tomato sauce

½ cup apple cider vinegar

⅓ cup honey

¼ cup molasses

¼ cup tomato paste

3 Tbsp. Worcestershire sauce

2 tsp. liquid smoke

2 garlic cloves, minced

1 Tbsp. dried minced onion

½ tsp. black pepper

½ tsp. kosher salt

red pepper flakes, to taste

Root Beer Pulled Pork Sandwiches

 5 minutes 6½ hours Serves 6-8

The beauty of this recipe is that your slow cooker and a can of soda does most of the work for you. And while you can easily use a bottle of store-bought barbecue sauce, try making your own—this version is super simple and contains an ingredient list you can pronounce.

INSTRUCTIONS:

1. Place pork tenderloin in your slow cooker and pour root beer over the meat. Cover and cook on low 4–6 hours, or until the meat shreds easily with a fork.

2. To make your own sauce, whisk all ingredients together in a medium saucepan. Bring to a simmer over medium–high heat. Reduce heat to low, and simmer for 20 minutes, or until sauce is slightly thickened. Use immediately or refrigerate for up to 1 week.

3. Once meat is cooked, discard liquid. Shred meat and place it back in the slow cooker. Toss with barbecue sauce, and heat for an additional 30 minutes on low to warm through. Top with Classic Coleslaw (see page 98).

INGREDIENTS:

½ cup mayonnaise

2 Tbsp. apple cider vinegar

1½ tsp. sugar

½ tsp. celery seeds

salt and pepper, to taste

1 (16-oz.) bag shredded coleslaw mix

Classic Coleslaw

 5 minutes   n/a   Serves 8

A tasty coleslaw is simple to make, and only requires a few ingredients. And while it is a perfect side dish for summer potlucks, it is simply fabulous piled high on Root Beer Pulled Pork Sandwiches (see page 97). If you haven't tried eating your barbecue this way before, give it a try!

INSTRUCTIONS:

1. In a large bowl, whisk together mayonnaise, apple cider vinegar, sugar, celery seeds, and salt and pepper. Add coleslaw mix and stir to combine, making sure dressing is incorporated throughout.

2. Refrigerate salad for at least 1 hour (or longer) prior to serving. Stir again before serving.

INGREDIENTS:

TOPPING:

½ cup flour

½ cup old-fashioned oats

½ cup light brown sugar

½ tsp. cinnamon

dash salt

4 Tbsp. butter, cut into chunks

FILLING:

3 Granny Smith apples, peeled and sliced thin

3 Tbsp. butter, melted

2 Tbsp. flour

1 Tbsp. orange juice

1 tsp. orange zest

½ tsp. vanilla extract

¼ cup light brown sugar

½ tsp. cinnamon

1 (6-oz.) pkg. fresh blackberries

Apple-Blackberry Crisp

 20 minutes   40–45 minutes   **S** Serves 8

Brown sugar and cinnamon-spiced apples are mixed with fresh blackberries and baked with a sweet oat crumble in this comforting, easier-than-pie dessert. It's especially wonderful served warm with vanilla bean ice cream.

INSTRUCTIONS:

1. Preheat oven to 350°F.

2. Spray an 8 × 8 pan with nonstick spray, and place peeled and sliced apples in prepared pan. Set aside.

3. Combine flour, oats, brown sugar, cinnamon, and salt in a medium bowl. Cut in the butter with 2 forks or a pastry blender until the mixture resembles coarse crumbs. Refrigerate until ready to use.

4. In a small bowl, combine melted butter and flour until well blended. Add orange juice, zest, and vanilla. Stir well. Then stir in brown sugar and cinnamon. Pour mixture over apples and toss to coat. Arrange blackberries over the top.

5. Sprinkle crumb topping evenly over fruit, and bake 40–45 minutes, or until the apples are tender and the top is golden brown. Serve warm with vanilla ice cream, if desired.

INGREDIENTS:

2 lbs. salmon

2 lemons, thinly sliced

6 sprigs fresh rosemary

kosher salt and black pepper

3 garlic cloves, minced

1 Tbsp. olive oil

Lemon-Rosemary Salmon

 10 minutes   15-20 minutes   Serves 6

If you've been hesitant to prepare fish at home, this method is easy and no-fuss. Even better: it requires very little cleanup. And by cooking your salmon in foil, you'll trap the moisture inside and keep your fish from drying out.

INSTRUCTIONS:

1. Preheat oven to 375°F.

2. Line a baking sheet with foil, making sure you have enough to enclose salmon on all four sides.

3. Arrange half of prepared lemon slices on the bottom of the foil. Layer with 3 sprigs of rosemary, and top with salmon. Sprinkle generously with salt and pepper and minced garlic, and layer with remaining rosemary and lemon slices. Drizzle with olive oil.

4. Fold the sides of the foil over sides of salmon, making sure the fish is completely covered.

5. Bake for 15–20 minutes or until fish flakes easily with a fork.

INGREDIENTS:

2½ cups chicken broth

1 cup uncooked white rice

1 garlic clove, minced

1 Tbsp. lemon zest

2 Tbsp. fresh dill

2 Tbsp. lemon juice

salt and pepper

Lemon-Dill Rice

 5 minutes   20-30 minutes   Serves 4

Jazz up plain white rice by adding fresh dill, garlic, and lemon juice in this easy-to-make side dish. While it pairs perfectly with seafood, we also enjoy it as a side dish with Honey Mustard Pork Tenderloin (see page 61).

INSTRUCTIONS:

1. Combine chicken broth, rice, and garlic in a medium saucepan. Bring to a boil; cover and reduce heat. Cook on low for 20–30 minutes or until liquid is absorbed.

2. Add zest, dill, and lemon juice. Fluff with a fork. Salt and pepper to taste. Serve immediately.

INGREDIENTS:

4-6 slices bacon

1 lb. fresh green beans

SAUCE:

1 tsp. sugar

2 Tbsp. balsamic vinegar

salt and pepper, to taste

INGREDIENTS:

2 Tbsp. butter

1 medium red onion, finely sliced

3-4 garlic cloves, minced

Balsamic Glazed Green Beans with Onions and Bacon

 15 minutes   20 minutes   Serves 6

Growing up, green beans were always my least favorite vegetable—but this side dish puts green beans out of a can to shame. In this easy recipe, fresh green beans are sautéed with caramelized onions and bacon, and are finished with a balsamic glaze. Your family is sure to request seconds.

INSTRUCTIONS:

1. Begin by frying your bacon in a large skillet. Boil a large pot of water. Rinse the beans in a colander and snap off ends. Snap beans in half and set aside.

2. Prepare sauce by mixing sugar, balsamic vinegar, and salt and pepper. Set aside.

3. Finish cooking bacon. Remove bacon from pan and allow to cool. Once cool, crumble it.

4. Drain all but 1 tablespoon of bacon grease, and add 2 tablespoons butter. Add onions and garlic, and stir.

5. Add beans to boiling water, and boil for just 1 minute. When the beans are still bright green, drain them in a clean colander.

6. Add the drained beans to the onions and garlic, and stir. Cook for another 2–3 minutes. Pour sauce on top of beans and allow to cook another few minutes, until beans are glazed. Add crumbled bacon to the beans and toss.

7. Allow beans to stand for a few minutes prior to serving. The glaze will thicken on standing.

Slow Cooker Pork Carnitas

 10 minutes 8 hours Serves 8

I love crispy pork carnitas. But let's face it—who really has time to spend babysitting them for hours in the oven to get that crispy goodness? By letting your slow cooker do the hard work—and then letting your broiler finish things off—you can have crispy carnitas with hardly any work!

INGREDIENTS:

5 garlic cloves, roughly chopped

1 Tbsp. chili powder

2 tsp. cumin

2 tsp. oregano

1 Tbsp. salt

1 tsp. pepper

4-5 lb. pork shoulder

2 oranges, juiced

2 limes, juiced

1 (14.5-oz.) can chicken broth

½ cup salsa

INSTRUCTIONS:

1. In a small bowl, combine garlic, chili powder, cumin, oregano, salt, and pepper to make a rub. Press mixture onto all sides of pork. Place meat into slow cooker.

2. Add orange juice, lime juice, chicken broth, and salsa. Cover and cook on low for 8 hours or on high 4–5 hours.

3. While meat is still in the slow cooker, shred with two forks. It should fall apart easily when it is ready.

4. Preheat broiler and line a baking sheet with aluminum foil. Place shredded meat on foil and drizzle a little sauce from the slow cooker over the top. Broil 5–10 minutes or until the edges of the meat just start to brown and crisp.

5. Serve on tortillas and with your favorite toppings: shredded cheese, fresh salsa (see page 8), chopped cilantro, and a dollop of sour cream.

INGREDIENTS:

3½ cups flour, plus more for dusting

¾ cup vegetable shortening or lard

2 tsp. kosher salt

1 cup lukewarm water

Homemade Flour Tortillas

 5 minutes   20-30 minutes   Makes 12 8-inch tortillas

If you haven't tried making your own tortillas before—you're missing out! They really aren't difficult at all, and once you taste them, you'll vow never to go back to store-bought again.

INSTRUCTIONS:

1. In a large bowl, blend flour and shortening until mixture is crumbly.

2. In a small bowl, mix salt and water until salt has dissolved. Using a stand mixer with a dough hook attachment, gradually add water to flour mixture, mixing until liquid is incorporated and the dough is smooth. If you do not have a stand mixer, stir liquid into flour mixture with a wooden spoon and then knead by hand.

3. Turn dough onto a floured surface and separate into 12 equal pieces. Roll each piece into a ball. Roll the balls as thinly as possible into (approximately) 8–inch circles.

4. Heat a griddle over moderately high heat. Place a raw tortilla on hot griddle and cook, turning twice, 1–1½ minutes each side, or until puffed and golden on both sides.

5. Wrap the cooked tortillas in a clean kitchen towel to keep warm. Serve immediately or allow to cool before storing in a container in the refrigerator.

INGREDIENTS:

1 Tbsp. butter

1 jalapeño, diced

2 garlic cloves, minced

1 tsp. chili powder

½ tsp. cumin

¼ tsp. salt

⅛ tsp. black pepper

1 Tbsp. flour

½ cup milk

 10 oz. white American cheese, shredded (you can find this at the deli counter)

6 oz. Pepper Jack cheese, shredded

1 Roma tomato, seeds removed and diced

⅓ cup chopped fresh cilantro

Homemade Queso Dip

 pt 5 minutes   **ct** 5 minutes   **s** Makes 2 cups

Queso dip is one of the most popular appetizers around. Who doesn't love that gooey, creamy cheese, perfect for dipping nachos (or . . .um, fingers?). I don't know about you, but I always hesitate to pop open a jar of that orange-colored queso dip you can purchase at the grocery store. Do yourself a favor and make your own—but make plenty. It will disappear in a flash!

INSTRUCTIONS:

1. Melt butter in a large saucepan over medium–high heat. Add jalapeño and garlic, and cook until softened.

2. Whisk in chili powder, cumin, salt, pepper, and flour. Add milk, whisking constantly to fully incorporate. Allow mixture to cook until slightly reduced, about 2 minutes.

3. Remove the pan from the heat and stir in shredded cheeses until melted.

4. Stir in tomatoes and chopped cilantro. Serve immediately. If serving at a party or gathering, keep your dip warm by serving it in a slow cooker to keep the cheese melted.

INGREDIENTS:

2 lbs. lean ground beef

1 lb. ground sausage

1 medium yellow onion, diced

2 Tbsp. minced garlic

2 (14-oz.) cans chicken broth

2 (15-oz.) cans chili beans, undrained

1 (8-oz.) can tomato sauce

1 (7-oz.) can diced green chilies

½ cup homemade chili seasoning (see below)

CHILI SEASONING:

½ cup chili powder

¼ cup ground cumin

2 Tbsp. garlic salt

2 Tbsp. dried oregano

1 Tbsp. ground coriander

1 tsp. crushed red pepper flakes, to taste

Easy Weeknight Chili

 30 minutes   30 minutes + **S** Serves 8

My dad has been participating in state chili cook-offs for over twenty years, and he's qualified for the world cook-off eight times— he definitely makes a mean bowl of chili! While he won't share his contest recipe, this version is the one I like to make at home. You can make it on the stovetop—but my favorite way to prepare it is to brown the meat the night before and let everything simmer in the slow cooker the next day for an easy meal after work.

INSTRUCTIONS:

1. Crumble beef and sausage in a Dutch oven, and cook over medium heat. Add diced onion and continue cooking until meat is no longer pink and onion is translucent. Add minced garlic and cook for one more minute.

2. Add chicken broth, beans, tomato sauce, green chilies, and chili seasoning to the pot, and bring to a low boil. Reduce heat to low and allow chili to simmer for a minimum of 30 minutes. If you have time to cook it longer, do so—the longer it simmers the better it tastes.

3. For a make–ahead version, transfer the cooked meat mixture to a slow cooker and add remaining ingredients. Cook on low 6–8 hours, or on high 3–4 hours.

* The homemade chili seasoning makes this chili extraordinary—so be sure to skip the packages and use this instead. Just add all ingredients to an airtight container, and shake to combine. This recipe makes about 1 cup (enough for two batches of this chili), and will keep for about 6 months in an airtight container stored at room temperature.

INGREDIENTS:

1 cup flour

1 cup yellow cornmeal

1 Tbsp. baking powder

½ cup sugar

1 tsp. salt

1 cup buttermilk*

2 large eggs

4 Tbsp. butter, melted

½ cup honey

¼ cup shredded cheddar cheese

2 jalapeños, diced

Cheesy Jalapeño Corn Muffins

 10 minutes   15 minutes   Makes 12 muffins

We love a good corn muffin, and these don't take much more time than stirring together a box mix. The combination of the honey and jalapeños adds just the right mixture of spicy to sweet, and, well . . . who doesn't love cheese? These muffins are great warm with a bit more honey drizzled over the top. And if jalapeños aren't your thing, substitute 2-3 tablespoons of diced scallions instead.

INSTRUCTIONS:

1. Preheat oven to 400°F. Spray a 12–cup muffin tin with nonstick cooking spray or line with paper muffin cups.

2. Combine flour, cornmeal, baking powder, sugar, and salt in a large bowl. In a smaller bowl, whisk together buttermilk, eggs, butter, and honey. Add egg mixture to flour mixture, and stir until just combined. Stir in cheese and diced jalapeños.

3. Evenly divide mixture between 12 prepared muffin tin cups. Bake for 15 minutes, or until golden.

   * Don't have buttermilk? No problem! Just pour 1 tablespoon of vinegar (or lemon juice) into a 1–cup measuring cup, and fill the remainder with milk. Allow the milk–vinegar mixture to sit at room temperature for 10 minutes, and then substitute for the buttermilk as listed above.

INGREDIENTS:

CAKE:

2 cups flour

1 tsp. baking powder

1 tsp. baking soda

1 cup sugar

4 Tbsp. unsweetened cocoa

1 cup mayonnaise

1 cup cold water

1 tsp. vanilla

FROSTING:

6 Tbsp. butter, softened

1/3 cup unsweetened cocoa

2 2/3 cup confectioner's sugar

1/3 cup milk

1 tsp. vanilla

sprinkles (optional)

Cheaper-than-a-Box-Mix Chocolate Cake with Fudge Buttercream

 10 minutes   35 minutes   **S** Serves 12

The primary reason I love baking this cake is that it requires only one bowl. Fewer dishes to wash is always a bonus in my kitchen! In addition, since it uses no eggs, it's quite economical to make, and doesn't require much more work than opening the box mixes you buy at the store. And the fudge buttercream? I could just eat it with a spoon!

INSTRUCTIONS:

1. Preheat oven to 350°F.

2. In a large bowl, whisk together flour, baking powder, baking soda, sugar, and cocoa. With a rubber spatula, stir in mayonnaise, cold water, and vanilla until combined. Pour batter into a 9 × 13 pan sprayed with nonstick cooking spray and bake for 35 minutes, or until a toothpick inserted in center comes out clean. Remove pan to wire rack, and allow cake to cool completely before frosting.

FOR THE FROSTING:

1. Beat butter in a large bowl with an electric mixer. Add cocoa and confectioner's sugar alternately with milk, beating to spreading consistency. Blend in vanilla—then frost. Garnish with sprinkles, if desired.

INGREDIENTS:

1 lb. lean ground beef

1 medium red onion, diced

½ green bell pepper, diced

1 clove garlic, minced

½ large bunch celery, chopped (including the leaves)

salt and pepper

1 (8-oz.) can sliced mushrooms

1 (46-oz.) can tomato juice

1 (28-oz.) can diced tomatoes

1 (3.5-oz.) pkg. sliced pepperoni, quartered

1 (15-oz.) can kidney beans, undrained

1 Tbsp. dried oregano

1 Tbsp. dried basil

¼-½ tsp. red pepper flakes

30-Minute Italian Chili

 10 minutes   20 minutes   Serves 15-20

This recipe has been a family favorite for over thirty years—and for good reason! It is quick and easy to make, serves a crowd, and is even better left over. It's perfect for an easy weeknight dinner, and is tasty enough to serve to company. We enjoy this hearty soup during crisp and cool fall evenings while game-watching with friends.

INSTRUCTIONS:

1. In a large stockpot, combine beef, onion, green pepper, and garlic until the meat is no longer pink. Add chopped celery, and sauté until celery becomes translucent. Add salt and pepper to taste.

2. Add remaining ingredients and simmer, stirring occasionally, for approximately 20 minutes.

   * This soup may be prepared in advance and then refrigerated and reheated. The flavors blend on standing, and it is even better the next day!

INGREDIENTS:

1½ cups warm water

2 Tbsp. sugar

1 Tbsp. fast-acting yeast

3½ cups flour, plus an additional ¼ cup if necessary.

1 tsp. salt

PARMESAN-BASIL BUTTER:

2 Tbsp. butter, melted

2 Tbsp. grated Parmesan cheese

¾ tsp. garlic powder

1 Tbsp. chopped fresh basil

¼ tsp. kosher salt

Parmesan-Basil Garlic Knots

 pt 30 minutes   ct 15-20 minutes   s Serves 15

There is not much better than homemade bread! And when that bread is brushed with a buttery blend of Parmesan, basil, and garlic, it is nearly impossible to resist. If you are new to working with yeast, this recipe is a great place to start. It requires very little hands-on time, only a few minutes of rise time, and is practically foolproof!

INSTRUCTIONS:

1. Preheat oven to 400°F. Spray a large baking sheet with nonstick spray or line with parchment paper.

2. Mix warm water, sugar, and yeast together in a large bowl. Stir together and let the mixture sit for 5 minutes, or until the yeast starts to get foamy.

3. Combine flour and salt with yeast mixture in the bowl of a stand mixer fitted with the dough hook attachment. Knead together until dough forms a soft ball. If you do not have a dough hook, you may knead mixture together with floured hands. If dough seems too sticky, add a bit more flour, a tablespoon at a time, up to ¼ cup. Allow dough to rise for 10 minutes.

4. Turn dough out onto a floured surface and divide into thirds. Cut each section into 5 equal pieces. Roll each small piece into 8—inch long ropes with your hands. Tie each rope into a knot, tucking one end on top and one end on bottom.

5. Place knots on a greased or parchment—lined baking sheet and allow them to rise for another 10 minutes.

6. Bake knots 15—20 minutes, or until golden.

7. While knots are baking, combine melted butter, cheese, garlic powder, basil, and salt. Brush butter mixture onto rolls as soon as they come out of the oven. Serve immediately.

INGREDIENTS:

¾ cup graham cracker crumbs

1 Tbsp. sugar

3 Tbsp. unsalted butter, melted

1 cup heavy cream

1 (8-oz.) pkg. cream cheese, room temperature

¾ cup sugar

2 Tbsp. lemon juice

1 tsp. lemon zest

1½ tsp. vanilla extract

1 (20-oz.) can cherry pie filling

Individual No-Bake Cherry Cheesecakes

 10 minutes n/a Serves 6

Cheesecake is one our favorite desserts—and when you don't have to bake it? Well, that's even better!

INSTRUCTIONS:

1. In a medium bowl, stir together graham cracker crumbs, 1 tablespoon sugar, and melted butter. Evenly divide the crumbs between serving dishes and press into the bottoms to form a crust.

2. Using an electric mixer with a whisk attachment, whisk heavy cream on medium–high speed until stiff peaks form.

3. In another bowl, beat cream cheese, ¾ cup sugar, lemon juice, lemon zest, and vanilla extract with a paddle attachment until smooth. Using a rubber spatula, carefully fold whipped cream into filling mixture.

4. Evenly spoon filling mixture into each glass and layer with cherry (or your favorite) pie filling.

5. Serve chilled.

INGREDIENTS:

6 large potatoes, peeled and cubed

1 large onion, diced

1 qt. (32 oz.) chicken broth or vegetable broth

3 garlic cloves, minced

¼ cup butter

1½ tsp. Herbes de Provence

1 tsp. dried parsley

1 tsp. marjoram

salt and pepper, to taste

1 cup whole milk or half-and-half

1 cup shredded cheese

for garnish: green onion, crumbled bacon, additional cheese

Slow Cooker Potato Soup

 15 minutes   8 hours   Serves 8

This potato soup is creamy and comforting, and requires little effort—it's the perfect weeknight meal for a chilly night! I love using Herbes de Provence in my potato soup—it's a wonderful blend of flavors, including rosemary, basil, and lavender, among others. You should be able to locate it in the spice aisle at your local market. If you do not have Herbes de Provence, for this recipe, you may substitute a half teaspoon each rosemary, thyme, and oregano.

INSTRUCTIONS:

1. Combine all ingredients except for the milk and cheese in your slow cooker.

2. Cook on high for 4 hours, or on low for 8 hours. Mash potatoes with a potato masher until they are coarsely chopped and soup is slightly thickened.

3. Stir in milk or half-and-half and cheese. Cook until milk is warmed through and the cheese is melted, about 2 minutes. Garnish as desired.

INGREDIENTS:

1 cup old-fashioned oats

2 cups boiling water

3 Tbsp. unsalted butter

²/₃ cup brown sugar

1 Tbsp. sugar

1½ tsp. salt

2 pkgs. yeast, softened in ⅓ cup warm water

5 cups flour, divided

Grandma's Oatmeal Rolls

 2 hours   20-30 minutes   Makes 18

My grandmother made these oatmeal rolls every year at Thanksgiving and Christmas—you could always find my dad and my uncles hanging out in the kitchen waiting for these rolls to come out of the oven. As with most homemade breads, these rolls always disappeared fast.

INSTRUCTIONS:

1. Preheat oven to 350°F. Combine oats, water, and butter in a medium saucepan. Cook over medium heat until softened, about 5 minutes. Remove from heat and let cool until lukewarm. Add brown sugar, sugar, salt, and yeast–water mixture.

2. In a large mixing bowl or the bowl of a stand mixer fitted with the dough hook, combine oat mixture with 3 cups flour. Gradually add remaining flour to form a dough—dough should be tacky to the touch but not overly sticky. If you do not have a stand mixer, you may combine ingredients together by hand with a wooden spoon or large rubber spatula.

3. Transfer dough to a lightly floured surface and knead until smooth. Place dough into a lightly oiled bowl and toss to coat. Cover dough with a clean kitchen towel and allow to rise in a warm spot until doubled in size, 40–60 minutes.

4. Divide dough into 3 equal parts, and then form each part into 6 rolls. Place rolls on a large jelly roll pan sprayed with nonstick cooking spray. Cover and place in a warm place to rise for an additional hour, or until the dough doubles in size.

5. Bake for 20–30 minutes, or until golden brown. Brush tops with melted butter, and serve warm.

INGREDIENTS:

CRUST:

8 Tbsp. butter, softened

¼ cup sugar

2 cups flour

pinch salt

FILLING:

½ cup sugar

2 Tbsp. flour

½ cup lemon juice

3 large eggs

1 cup fresh raspberries

powdered sugar, for dusting

Lemon-Raspberry Squares

 10 minutes   45 minutes   Makes 9 generous squares

Sweet, tangy, decadent, and gooey—lemon bars are just a classic. With a perfectly buttery crust and a creamy lemon filling studded with fresh raspberries, these Lemon Raspberry Squares will be your new favorite. Get ready to pucker up!

INSTRUCTIONS:

1. Preheat oven to 350°F. Line an 8 × 8 baking pan with parchment or foil and lightly spray with nonstick cooking spray.

2. For the crust, cream butter and sugar together with an electric mixer. Mix in flour and salt until dough forms. Press dough into prepared pan. Bake 15–20 minutes or until the crust is lightly golden. Chill.

3. Reduce the oven temperature to 325°F. Whisk together filling ingredients, except raspberries and powdered sugar, until smooth. Arrange fresh raspberries over baked crust and pour filling over the top.

4. Bake 22–25 minutes or until filling has set. Allow bars to cool completely on a wire rack. Dust with powdered sugar when serving.

INGREDIENTS:

1 Tbsp. olive oil

1 small onion, diced (I used a red one)

1 cup diced bell pepper (any color or a combination)

4-5 garlic cloves, minced

2 cups Fiesta-Lime Chicken (see page 25)

1 (10-oz.) can diced tomatoes and green chilies

3 Tbsp. tomato paste

1 (32-oz.) can chicken stock

2 cups salsa

1 (15-oz.) can black beans, drained

1 (15-oz.) can corn, drained

3 Tbsp. cornmeal

To garnish: lime, tortilla chips, sour cream, shredded cheese, tomatoes, cilantro, pico de gallo

Chicken Tortilla Soup

 15 minutes   1 hour   Serves 6

This chicken tortilla soup is easy to throw together, full of flavor, and perfect for warming up on a cold night! If you like Mexican flavors, you're going to love this soup!

INSTRUCTIONS:

1. Heat oil in a heavy-bottomed soup pot over medium-high heat. Add onion, bell pepper, and garlic. Stir to combine. Cook 1–2 minutes, and then add Fiesta-Lime Chicken.

2. Pour in diced tomatoes and green chilies, tomato paste, chicken stock, salsa, black beans, and corn. Stir to combine and allow soup to come to a boil. Reduce heat and simmer 30–45 minutes, uncovered.

3. Meanwhile, mix cornmeal with a small amount of water. Pour cornmeal mixture into soup, and then allow to simmer 30 additional minutes.

4. If you're using your own seasoned chicken and not the Fiesta-Lime Chicken, check your seasonings as you go—you may want to add in additional chili powder, cumin, and salt.

5. Garnish as desired. Optional: I sometimes squeeze in a bit of lime juice just prior to serving.

INGREDIENTS:

½ cup sour cream

½ cup mayonnaise

¼ cup chopped cilantro

juice of ½ lime

1 (10-oz.) can diced tomatoes and green chilies, drained

1 (15-oz.) can corn, drained

1 (4-oz.) can diced green chilies

1 cup shredded cheddar cheese

Cilantro-Lime Mexi-Corn Dip

 5 minutes   2 hours chill time   Makes approximately 3 cups

This easy dip is a family favorite. I first got the recipe from my cousin, and it now makes an appearance at every family function we have.

INSTRUCTIONS:

1. Mix all ingredients together in a medium bowl, stirring to combine. Refrigerate at least 2 hours prior to serving.

INGREDIENTS:

2¼ cups flour

1½ tsp. baking powder

½ tsp. baking soda

½ tsp. salt

1 tsp. cinnamon

4 Tbsp. butter, softened

¾ cup sugar

¼ cup light brown sugar

3 medium bananas, mashed

1 cup vanilla yogurt

2 eggs

¾ tsp. almond extract

¾ tsp. vanilla extract

1 cup mini chocolate chips

2 Tbsp. raw sugar

Cinnamon-Banana Chocolate Chip Muffins

 20 minutes   25 minutes   Makes 18 muffins

If you're like me, you almost always have overripe bananas hanging out on your kitchen counter. Put those guys to use by whipping up some of these Banana Chocolate Chip Muffins (or try the Raspberry Mango Smoothie on page 185). These are perfect for an after-dinner snack or a grab-and-go breakfast. I love sprinkling mine with sugar-in-the-raw (also known as turbinado or raw sugar; you can find this in the baking aisle in your grocery store), but that is completely optional.

INSTRUCTIONS:

1. Preheat oven to 350°F. Line muffin tins with baking cups or cupcake liners.

2. In a medium bowl, whisk together dry ingredients: flour, baking powder, baking soda, salt, and cinnamon. Set aside

3. In a larger bowl, cream together butter, sugar, and brown sugar. Add in mashed bananas, yogurt, eggs, and extracts, and mix well. Gradually add flour mixture to combine. Stir in chocolate chips.

4. Using a ¼-cup measuring cup, pour batter into muffin tins. Sprinkle tops with raw sugar. Bake 20–25 minutes, or until muffins are just golden brown.

INGREDIENTS:

2 Tbsp. olive oil

3 lbs. chuck roast

kosher salt and fresh ground pepper

2½ cups beef broth

¼ cup pickle juice

1 lb. baby carrots

2 lbs. potatoes, chopped into 2-inch pieces

1 large yellow onion, cut into chunks

2-3 sprigs fresh thyme

2-3 sprigs fresh rosemary

Beef Roast with Veggies

 20 minutes   9 hours   **s** Serves 6

Beef roast with carrots and potatoes was a staple in my house growing up, and I think everyone should have a go-to recipe for this easy, comforting meal. My dad and my husband both still go googly-eyed when they find out this recipe is on the meal plan for the week. Although I've tweaked my mom's recipe over the years, I still include her "secret" ingredient: pickle juice.

INSTRUCTIONS:

1. Heat olive oil in a large skillet over medium–high heat. Season roast liberally with salt and pepper, and sear for about 1 minute on all sides until nice and brown. Remove roast and place it in your slow cooker.

2. Add broth and pickle juice, making sure there is enough liquid to cover the roast at least halfway. Add carrots, potatoes, onion, thyme, and rosemary.

3. Put the lid on and cook on high for 6 hours or on low for 9 hours.

4. Place roast on a large plate or serving platter. Use a fork to gently pull apart roast. Serve with carrots and potatoes.

INGREDIENTS:

1 pkg. active dry yeast (2¼ tsp.)

½ cup warm water

1 cup cottage cheese, room temperature

2 Tbsp. sugar

¼ cup minced dried onion

1 Tbsp. butter, melted

2 Tbsp. dried dill weed

1 tsp. salt

¼ tsp. baking soda

1 egg

2¼-3 cups flour

Cottage Cheese Dill Bread

 1 hour and 45 minutes 45 minutes **S** Makes 1 loaf

There's virtually nothing I love more than a loaf of homemade bread, fresh and hot from the oven. It's a bit dangerous for me, though, because I can easily eat the entire loaf myself, and this recipe is no exception. This Cottage Cheese Dill Bread recipe was given to my mom from an old family friend—which she fortunately passed down to me. Even though the recipe uses cottage cheese (normally a turnoff for me) you can't taste it. The result is a soft, but hearty bread, which is the perfect accompaniment for Beef Roast with Veggies (page 139).

INSTRUCTIONS:

1. In a small bowl, sprinkle yeast over warm water and let stand for 5 minutes, or until the yeast is foamy and dissolved.

2. In a large mixing bowl, combine cottage cheese, sugar, minced onion, butter, dill weed, salt, baking soda, egg, and yeast water.

3. Add flour in portions, beating after each addition to form a stiff ball. Cover the bowl with a clean kitchen towel and let rise until doubled in size, about 1 hour.

4. Punch dough down and place into a well–greased loaf pan. Let rise for another 30–40 minutes.

5. Preheat oven to 350°F. Bake 40–45 minutes. Brush with butter and sprinkle with kosher salt.

INGREDIENTS:

¼ cup butter

2 tsp. lemon juice

½ cup water

4 large apples, peeled, cored and sliced

¼ cup red hots

3 tsp. cornstarch

2 Tbsp. water

2 Tbsp. brown sugar

½ tsp. cinnamon

Red Hot Cinnamon Apples

 10 minutes 15 minutes Serves 4

These sautéed cinnamon apples are one of my son's favorite treats. They are so easy to make, and the addition of the melted red hots make them extra special—even for adults!

INSTRUCTIONS:

1. Melt butter in a large skillet over medium heat. Add lemon juice, water, apples, and red hots. Sauté until apples are tender and red hots are melted, stirring constantly, 5–7 minutes.

2. In a small bowl, combine cornstarch with 2 tablespoons water. Stir cornstarch mixture into apples.

3. Stir in brown sugar and cinnamon. Boil for 2 minutes, stirring occasionally.

4. Remove from heat and serve warm.

INGREDIENTS:

16 toasted baguette slices

8 oz. whipped feta (see below)

16 slices thinly sliced prosciutto

2 fresh peaches, sliced thin

honey, for drizzling

WHIPPED FETA:

8 oz. feta cheese

3 oz. whipped cream cheese, room temperature

Peach and Prosciutto Crostini with Whipped Feta

 10 minutes n/a Serves 8

If you've never had whipped feta, you need to change that pronto. I love feta cheese, but quite frankly, crumbly feta can be a pain to eat. But creaming feta with whipped cream cheese takes feta to a new level—and opens up a whole new world of serving opportunities. Smear a bit on some toasted baguette slices and layer with fresh peaches and prosciutto for a quick and easy appetizer. This would be equally fabulous with fresh figs and prosciutto.

INSTRUCTIONS:

1. Spread each slice of toasted bread with whipped feta. Top with a slice of prosciutto, 2 peach slices, and a drizzle of honey. Serve immediately.

FOR WHIPPED FETA:

1. Combine feta and whipped cream cheese in a food processor and puree until creamy, scraping down the sides of the bowl as needed.

INGREDIENTS:

1 Tbsp. olive oil

1 red onion, diced

3 garlic cloves, diced

½ tsp. red pepper flakes

½ tsp. crushed fennel seeds

2 (32-oz.) containers low-sodium chicken stock

1 (14.5-oz.) can fire-roasted diced tomatoes

2 Tbsp. tomato paste or leftover Quick Pizza Sauce (see page 164)

1 lb. chicken breasts

1½ tsp. Italian seasoning

1 tsp. parsley

1 tsp. thyme

8 oz. ditalini or other small pasta

½ cup grated Parmesan

salt and pepper

Chicken-Parmesan Soup

 10 minutes   30 minutes   Serves 8

I have to admit, a hearty bowl of soup that you can prepare on a weeknight in just about 30 minutes is right up my alley. This soup has all of the same flavors of the Baked Chicken Parmesan (see page 43), but comes in an even leaner vehicle. Chicken broth and fire-roasted tomatoes are simmered with onion, garlic, fennel, red pepper flakes, and lots of lovely spices for a wonderfully aromatic base. The perfectly boiled chicken along with ditalini pasta will keep you full. And, of course, don't forget the gooey cheese!

INSTRUCTIONS:

1. Heat oil in a large stockpot over medium heat. Add onion and cook until translucent, about 5 minutes. Add garlic, pepper flakes, and fennel, and cook another minute, just until fragrant.

2. Add chicken stock, diced tomatoes, tomato paste, chicken breasts, Italian seasoning, parsley, and thyme. Bring to a boil. Reduce the heat and simmer for 10 minutes.

3. Add pasta and cook for 10 minutes longer, or until pasta is al dente, or still just slightly firm.

4. Remove chicken from liquid; shred it and return it to the stockpot. Stir in Parmesan until melted. Season with salt and pepper, to taste.

INGREDIENTS:

1½ cups flour

1½ cups quick cooking oats

1 cup brown sugar

1 tsp. baking powder

¾ cup unsalted butter

1 jar apricot jam (I used a 15.5-oz. jar)

Apricot Jam Bars

 15 minutes   30 minutes   Makes 12 bars

My mom has been making these bars longer than I've been alive—so for more years than I'm willing to share. This is an old family recipe from my grandfather's cousin Kristine. I like eating these bars with a cup of coffee or tea in the morning (they do have oats in them, after all!), but they're just as good served as an after-school snack or as an after-dinner treat.

INSTRUCTIONS:

1. Preheat oven to 350°F. Spray a 9 × 9 baking dish with nonstick spray.

2. Combine flour, oats, sugar and baking powder in a large bowl. Cut in butter with a pastry blender or use 2 forks until the mixture resembles coarse crumbs.

3. Press ¾ of oat mixture into the prepared pan. Spread apricot jam over the oat mixture and top with remaining oat mixture.

4. Bake for 30 minutes or until bars are lightly golden.

INGREDIENTS:

8 oz. cream cheese, softened

1 cup mozzarella cheese, shredded

½ cup mayonnaise

4 garlic cloves, minced

½ tsp. dried basil

½ tsp. dried oregano

1 (14.5-oz.) can diced tomatoes, drained

 1 (7.5-oz.) jar artichoke hearts, drained and chopped

Artichoke Bruschetta Dip

 pt 10 minutes   ct 15-18 minutes   s Serves 6-8

This easy-to-make dip is loaded with cheese, garlic, tomatoes, and artichokes. Slather it on crusty bread slices or serve it with pita chips, crackers, or tortilla chips.

INSTRUCTIONS:

1. Preheat oven to 425°F. Spray an 8 × 8 baking dish with nonstick cooking spray and set aside.

2. Beat cream cheese with mixer until smooth. Stir in mozzarella, mayonnaise, garlic, spices, tomatoes, and artichoke hearts until well combined.

3. Spread mixture into prepared baking dish and bake 15–18 minutes or until bubbly and golden brown. Serve with chips or toasted bread slices.

INGREDIENTS:

VINAIGRETTE:

1 Tbsp. red wine vinegar

½ tsp. mayonnaise

½ tsp. dijon mustard

1 Tbsp. minced fresh oregano

⅛ tsp. kosher salt

⅛ tsp. pepper

3 Tbsp. olive oil

SALAD:

1 (10-oz.) bag American blend salad

4-6 pepperoncini peppers

 1 small tomato, quartered

¼ red onion, sliced thin

3 Tbsp. sliced black olives

½ cup large croutons

freshly grated Parmesan cheese

Italian Salad with Herb Vinaigrette

 25 minutes n/a Serves 4

This is my favorite salad to pair with Spaghetti and Meatballs (see page 155). The herb vinaigrette is what makes it so yummy! It's just a kicked-up version of that bottled Italian dressing sitting in your fridge door right now. It takes just a few minutes to make, and it doesn't have any weird, unpronounceable ingredients in it either.

INSTRUCTIONS:

1. Combine vinegar, mayonnaise, dijon, oregano, salt, and pepper. Whisk until no lumps remain. While whisking, stream olive oil constantly into vinegar mixture until glossy and thickened. Store for up to two weeks, covered, in the refrigerator.

2. Place salad ingredients in a large bowl and drizzle with dressing. Serve immediately.

INGREDIENTS:

MEATBALLS:

1 large egg

½ lb. ground beef

½ lb. ground sausage

¼ cup bread crumbs

2 Tbsp. grated Parmesan cheese

1 tsp. dried parsley

1 tsp. dried basil

1 tsp. dried oregano

¼ tsp. kosher salt

¼ tsp. pepper

½ tsp. garlic powder

SAUCE:

1 large yellow onion, chopped

2 (28-oz.) cans crushed tomatoes

4 garlic cloves, minced

1 Tbsp. dried basil

1 tsp. dried oregano

red pepper flakes, to taste

FOR SERVING: pasta, cheese, and basil

Homemade Spaghetti and Meatballs

 20 minutes   6 hours   Serves 6

To put it simply: nothing beats homemade spaghetti and meatballs. These meatballs are spiced perfectly—and when you can have them on your dinner table with hardly any work involved, that's a win for everyone. With this recipe, you can put your slow cooker to work and have a warm and comforting dinner ready to feed your family with little hands-on time.

INSTRUCTIONS:

1. Beat egg in a large mixing bowl. Add ground beef, sausage, bread crumbs, cheese, and spices. Stir to combine the ingredients, but do not overmix. Form mixture into desired sized balls (you may use a cookie scoop for consistency), and place on a foil–lined pan sprayed with nonstick cooking spray. Broil the meatballs just until they start to brown—you're not cooking them all the way through.

2. Place chopped onion in the bottom of your slow cooker, and place lightly browned meatballs on top of them. Add tomatoes, garlic, basil, oregano, and red pepper flakes. Cover and cook on low 5–6 hours or on high 3–4 hours.

3. Serve with pasta, and sprinkle with fresh Parmesan cheese and basil right before serving.

INGREDIENTS:

1 lb. hot Italian sausage

1 (8-oz.) pkg. cream cheese, softened to room temperature

1 (10-oz.) pkg. frozen spinach, thawed and squeezed dry

1 egg, lightly beaten

1 cup cottage cheese

2 cups shredded Italian blend cheese

2 cups shredded mozzarella cheese, divided

1 cup grated Parmesan cheese

¼ tsp. salt

¼ tsp. pepper

24 jumbo pasta shells, cooked and cooled

SAUCE:

1 (28-oz.) jar crushed tomatoes

2 Tbsp. dried parsley

2 Tbsp. dried basil

3 garlic cloves, minced

red pepper flakes, to taste

Sausage and Spinach-Stuffed Shells

 30 minutes   55 minutes   Serves 10

Don't let the name fool you—my kiddo gobbles these up with no clue that these cheesy, sausage-stuffed shells even contain spinach. And who could blame him? With cream cheese, cottage cheese, and three types of cheeses, there is enough ooey, gooey goodness going on in this dish to keep your palate—and stomach—satisfied.

INSTRUCTIONS:

1. Preheat oven to 350°F. Spray a 9 × 13 baking dish with nonstick cooking spray.

2. Brown sausage in a large skillet over medium heat.

3. While sausage is browning, prepare sauce: combine tomatoes, parsley, basil, garlic, and red pepper flakes in a large bowl and mix well. Spoon ¼ cup sauce into the bottom of the baking dish.

4. Drain sausage and transfer to a large bowl. Combine sausage with cream cheese, thawed spinach, and egg. Stir well, and then add in the cottage cheese, Italian blend cheese, 1 cup mozzarella, Parmesan, and salt and pepper. Stir to combine.

5. Stuff cooked shells with sausage and cheese mixture and place in prepared pan. Spoon remaining sauce over shells. If needed, place any extra shells in an 8 × 8 baking dish.

6. Cover with foil and bake for 45 minutes. Uncover and sprinkle with remaining 1 cup mozzarella. Bake for an additional 5–10 minutes, or until cheese has melted. Let stand for 5 minutes before serving.

INGREDIENTS:

½ cup butter, softened

2 Tbsp. garlic powder

1½ tsp. dried oregano

1½ tsp. dried thyme

1 loaf French bread, halved horizontally

½ cup shredded Italian blend cheese

Cheesy Garlic Bread

 10 minutes   30 minutes   Serves 4

My husband loves the loaves of garlic bread you buy from your grocer that come pre-sliced and filled with seasoned butter. But it's just as easy to make your own at home—and this way, you can add lots of melted cheese. To get nice slices without pulling off the cheese, slice bread cheese side down with a serrated knife.

INSTRUCTIONS:

1. Adjust oven rack to lower–middle position and preheat to 400°F.

2. Mix butter, garlic powder, oregano, and thyme in a small bowl, and spread on cut sides of bread. Sandwich bread back together and wrap in foil. Place foil–wrapped bread on baking sheet and bake for 15 minutes.

3. Remove foil and place buttered sides up on baking sheet. Bake for 10 minutes, or until bread just begins to color. Remove bread from oven and set oven to broil.

4. Sprinkle bread with cheese and broil 1–2 minutes, or until cheese melts and starts to bubble.

INGREDIENTS:

1½ oz. blackberry syrup

crushed ice

6 oz. sparkling water or seltzer water

½ oz. half-and-half

Blackberry Italian Cream Sodas

 5 minutes   n/a   Serves 1

You don't have to go to a fancy restaurant or pay high prices to have an Italian cream soda at home. Not only are they simple to make, but they are an impressive crowd-pleaser. You can find fruit flavored syrups at many places: I find mine at my local spice merchant, but they are also available at World Market or Amazon, among others.

INSTRUCTIONS:

1. Pour blackberry syrup (or your favorite flavor) into the bottom of a glass. Fill the glass halfway with crushed ice and pour sparkling water over the top. Add half-and-half. Garnish with fresh fruit: cherries, lemons, limes, or berries.

INGREDIENTS:

3½–4 cups flour, divided

1 pkg. active dry yeast (2¼ tsp.)

½ tsp. garlic salt

1½ cups water

olive oil, for brushing on the crust prior to baking

kosher salt and ground black pepper, optional

Basic Pizza Dough

 pt 90 minutes   **ct** 20 minutes   **s** Makes two 12-inch crusts

When my husband was growing up, his family had homemade pizza night often. This is his mom's basic pizza dough recipe, and we use it now in our own home. Although the steps may look lengthy, it's really not that complicated. Most of the process is just wait time! And the results are well worth it—the fun thing about homemade pizza night is that everyone gets to pick their own toppings.

INSTRUCTIONS:

1. Warm the water to 120°F—just warm enough that you need to take your finger out when you stir the water.

2. In a large mixing bowl or the bowl of a stand mixer fitted with the dough hook, combine 2 cups flour, yeast, garlic salt, and warm water. Mix for 3 minutes. Gradually add remaining flour to form a moderately stiff dough. If you do not have a stand mixer, you may combine ingredients together by hand with a wooden spoon or large rubber spatula. If your dough does not form into a ball, add 1–2 teaspoons of water and mix again. Let dough rest 5–10 minutes, then mix again until the dough is tacky to the touch but not sticky.

3. Transfer your dough to a lightly floured surface and knead until smooth and satiny, or about 4 minutes. Place dough into a lightly oiled bowl and toss to coat. Cover dough with a clean kitchen towel and allow to rise in a warm spot until doubled in size, 40–60 minutes. You may speed this process up by bringing your oven to 200 degrees, turning it off, and placing the dough inside with the oven opened just slightly.

4. After dough has risen, turn it out onto a floured surface and punch it down. Divide dough into 2 equal pieces and shape each piece into a smooth ball.

5. Coat your hands lightly with olive oil. Shape dough into two 13-inch circles, folding the edge over the make a ridge to hold in sauce and fillings, and place on cookie sheets or on pizza pans. After you shape your dough, cover it and allow it to rise for 15 minutes. This step is important because this second rise allows your dough to develop some volume so that it does not bake up dense and heavy.

6. Next, lightly brush your crust with a bit of olive oil. I sometimes like to sprinkle my dough with a bit of extra kosher salt and pepper to help bring out the flavors of the crust.

7. Add your favorite sauce and fillings, and top with cheese. Bake at 450°F for 15–20 minutes, or until cheese has melted and crust is lightly golden.

FREEZING: This recipe makes enough dough for two 12-inch pizzas. If you wish to make just one pizza, you may freeze half. Shape and freeze wrap remaining crust; store in freezer up to 2 weeks. Defrost 20 minutes before baking.

INGREDIENTS:

1 (6-oz.) can tomato paste

6 oz. water

1 Tbsp. honey

½ tsp. red pepper flakes

¾ tsp. onion powder

1 Tbsp. Parmesan cheese

1 tsp. garlic powder

½ tsp. oregano

½ tsp. basil

Quick Pizza Sauce

 10 minutes   n/a   Covers 2 pizzas, see page 165

While a slow simmering pizza sauce is great, sometimes quick and easy is what you need in a pinch. This recipe is fabulous, and it also makes a great dipping sauce for breadsticks, or the Parmesan-Basil Garlic Knots (see page 122).

INSTRUCTIONS:

1. Combine all ingredients in a small bowl and mix to incorporate. Allow to stand until ready to use. Covers two pizzas (see Basic Pizza Dough, page 163). Freezes well.

INGREDIENTS:

½ recipe Basic Pizza Dough, page 163

½ recipe Quick Pizza Sauce, page 164

olive oil

kosher salt and black pepper, to taste

 1 tsp. Italian seasoning (optional)

8 oz. fresh mozzarella, sliced thin

1 (5-oz.) pkg. cooked ham or Canadian bacon

½ cup pineapple chunks

Hawaiian Pizza

 pt 2 hours   **ct** 20 minutes   **s** Serves 4

Make your next pizza night extra fun with this Hawaiian version: a combination of tomato sauce, mozzarella, ham, and pineapple chunks. Not only is it easy, it's a great way to use up leftover ham.

INSTRUCTIONS:

1. Preheat oven to 450°F.

2. Drizzle crust lightly with olive oil and sprinkle crust with kosher salt and pepper and Italian seasoning, if desired.

3. Top crust with sauce, and then layer with cheese, followed by Canadian bacon and pineapple

4. Bake 15–20 minutes, or until crust is lightly browned and cheese is bubbly.

INGREDIENTS:

2 Tbsp. olive oil

1 lb. smoked turkey sausage, sliced

5 garlic cloves, minced

2 roasted red peppers, sliced into thin strips

1 yellow bell pepper, diced

1 (28-oz.) can crushed tomatoes

1 cup chicken broth

1½ cups water

12 oz. rigatoni pasta

3 Tbsp. butter

2 tsp. chopped fresh basil

½ tsp. kosher salt

¼ cup heavy cream

1 cup Parmesan cheese

crushed red pepper flakes, to taste

Skillet Pasta with Turkey Sausage and Roasted Peppers

 10 minutes   45 minutes   (s) Serves 6

One-pot meals are basically my go-to for weeknight dinners. We love smoked sausage, and when paired with fragrant garlic, roasted red peppers, and tomatoes, it creates a one-skillet meal that is sure to please your whole family!

INSTRUCTIONS:

1. Add olive oil to a 4– or 5–quart sauté pan over medium–high heat. Add sausage, and cook until lightly browned. Add garlic, and cook for 30 seconds more.

2. Stir in the peppers, and sauté for another minute. Add in tomatoes, chicken broth, water, and pasta, and bring to a low boil, adding more water if necessary. Continue to cook, stirring frequently, until the pasta is cooked to al dente, 15–20 minutes.

3. Reduce the heat to low and add in the butter, basil, and salt. After the butter has melted, add the cream and cheese. Simmer for 10 minutes, stirring occasionally.

4. Serve warm, with additional cheese, chopped basil, and red pepper flakes, if desired.

INGREDIENTS:

1 (15-oz.) can garbanzo beans, drained

3 garlic cloves, roughly chopped

1 jalapeño, seeded and diced

1 cup cilantro, rinsed and roughly chopped

⅓ cup tahini

1 tsp. cumin

½ tsp. coriander

salt and pepper, to taste

1 lime, juiced

5-6 Tbsp. olive oil, or more as needed

Cilantro Jalapeño Hummus

 pt 10 minutes   **ct** n/a   **s** Makes about 2 cups

Hummus is one of my all-time favorite snacks. Between my husband and me, we can eat one of those ridiculously overpriced packages of hummus from the refrigerated section in one sitting . . . so we've started making our own hummus on a regular basis instead. It's easy, much more economical, and tastes so much better. Tahini is a must in hummus making; you can find it in the Mediterranean section of your grocery store.

INSTRUCTIONS:

1. Place all ingredients except for oil in the bowl of a food processor or in the jar of a heavy–duty blender. Process until smooth, and then add oil in a steady stream and process until desired consistency is reached. Chill for 1 hour before serving.

2. Serve with pita chips or fresh vegetables.

INGREDIENTS:

2 cups flour

½ tsp. salt

2 tsp. cinnamon

1 tsp. baking powder

1 tsp. baking soda

4 eggs, lightly beaten

2 cups sugar

1 cup vegetable oil

1 (15-oz.) can pumpkin

FROSTING:

3 oz. cream cheese, softened

2 cups powdered sugar

1 Tbsp. milk

1 tsp. vanilla

Grandma's Pumpkin Snack Cake

 20 minutes   30 minutes   Serves 18

This snack cake is packed full of fall flavors and topped with an easy cream cheese cinnamon-dusted frosting! I swiped this pumpkin snack cake recipe from my grandma's recipe box, although I think it's a pretty standard, popular pumpkin cake recipe. You'll find this recipe popular because this cake is so soft, super easy to make, and cinnamon-spicy good. Fall doesn't get much better than this.

INSTRUCTIONS:

1. Preheat oven to 350°F and spray a 9 × 13 pan with nonstick cooking spray.

2. In a medium bowl, stir together flour, salt, cinnamon, baking powder, and baking soda.

3. In the bowl of a stand mixer, combine eggs, sugar, oil, and pumpkin mix. Add dry ingredients to pumpkin mixture, and beat at low speed until combined and batter is smooth.

4. Spread batter into pan and bake for 30 minutes, or until a toothpick inserted in center comes out clean. Allow cake to cool completely before frosting.

5. To make the frosting, beat cream cheese with an electric mixer until smooth. Add in sugar and milk, and mix at low speed until combined. Stir in vanilla and mix again. Spread over cooled bars. Dust lightly with cinnamon, if desired.

INGREDIENTS:

2 Tbsp. olive oil

1 lb. chicken breasts, cut into 1-inch pieces

1 Tbsp. chili powder

1 tsp. cumin

½ tsp. coriander

1 tsp. garlic powder

salt and pepper, to taste

½ lime, juiced

1 batch enchilada sauce (see page 73) or 2 cups of your favorite store-bought enchilada sauce

1 (4-oz.) can green chilies, diced

²/₃ cup sour cream

12 oz. fusilli pasta, cooked according to package directions

6 small corn tortillas, cut into small pieces

1 cup shredded Mexican cheese

FOR SERVING: avocado, diced tomatoes, sliced olives, tortilla chips

Chicken Enchilada Pasta

 20 minutes   15 minutes   Serves 6

This pasta is like an enchilada in deconstructed form. Enchiladas are one of my favorite comfort foods (see Beef and Cheese Enchiladas on page 74), but combining all the flavors into a one-pot meal makes for an easy-breezy weeknight dinner. This pasta dish is so easy and customizable—try adding in some corn or black beans to up the veggie count or to make this a meatless meal. And if you'd like it extra spicy, just sauté a seeded and diced jalapeño or Serrano pepper along with your chicken.

INSTRUCTIONS:

1. Add olive oil to a 4- or 5-quart sauté pan over medium high heat. Add chicken pieces to pan and season with chili powder, cumin, coriander, garlic powder, salt, pepper, and lime juice. Cook for 8–10 minutes.

2. Add enchilada sauce, green chilies, and sour cream. Stir to combine. Stir in cooked pasta and tortillas. Add cheese and stir until melted. Top with avocado, diced tomatoes, sliced olives, and crunchy tortilla strips.

INGREDIENTS:

DRESSING:

3 Tbsp. freshly squeezed lime juice

2 garlic cloves, minced

½ tsp. kosher salt

½ tsp. sugar

¼ tsp. cumin

⅛ tsp. coriander

1 Tbsp. chopped cilantro

3 Tbsp. olive oil

SALAD:

1 large head Romaine lettuce, rinsed, chopped, and dried

1 cup corn

½ red onion, diced

1 avocado, diced

½ cucumber, sliced

1 cup cherry tomatoes, halved

¼ cup cilantro, chopped

FOR SERVING:

⅓ cup queso fresco

crunchy tortilla strips (optional)

Mexican Chopped Salad with Lime Vinaigrette

 20 minutes   n/a   Serves 4-6

This easy chopped salad is a fun spin on the regular old boring side salad. You can change up the vegetables according to your family's tastes—try adding black beans, snap peas, or a little jalapeño for some added heat. The vinaigrette mixes up in a flash and adds just the right amount of zing with lime juice, cumin, and cilantro.

INSTRUCTIONS:

1. Combine lime juice, garlic, salt, sugar, cumin, coriander, and cilantro in a small bowl. While whisking, stream olive oil constantly into mixture. Store for up to two weeks, covered, in the refrigerator.

2. Place all salad ingredients together in a large bowl. Drizzle with the dressing. Serve immediately.

INGREDIENTS:

1 Tbsp. cocoa powder

⅓ cup hot water

4 oz. bittersweet chocolate

7 oz. sweetened condensed milk

1 tsp. cinnamon

⅛ tsp. nutmeg

¼ tsp. chili powder

1 tsp. vanilla

4 cups milk

1 cup half-and-half or heavy cream

FOR SERVING:

whipped cream, marshmallows, and chocolate syrup

Mexican Spiced Hot Chocolate

 5 minutes   5 minutes   **s** Serves 4-6

Try a twist on the traditional hot chocolate by adding a pinch of chili powder. It's not strong enough to be spicy—it adds just the right amount of depth and flavor to the chocolate. This easy-to-make stovetop version is perfectly rich and creamy, thanks to the addition of sweetened condensed milk and a bit of heavy cream. It's not diet friendly, but as long as you don't drink it every night of the week, it makes for a wonderful special treat.

INSTRUCTIONS:

1. In a heavy-bottomed saucepan, combine cocoa powder and hot water. Whisk until smooth. Add remaining ingredients, and heat over medium heat until simmering, stirring frequently.

2. Remove from heat and serve with optional toppings.

INGREDIENTS:

2 Tbsp. butter

2 Tbsp. olive oil

2 medium red potatoes, diced into ½-inch pieces

1 bell pepper, diced (any color)

salt and pepper, to taste

½ cup chicken broth

1 lb. breakfast sausage

6 large eggs

¼ cup half-and-half (or whole milk)

1 tsp. dry mustard

1 tsp. seasoned salt

½ cup shredded cheddar cheese

½ cup pepper jack cheese

6 large flour tortillas

Loaded Breakfast Burritos

 20 minutes   25 minutes   S Serves 6

I'll admit it, sometimes we love having breakfast for dinner. While I'm more of the muffin and smoothie variety, these Loaded Breakfast Burritos are right up my husband's alley. That's because they have it all: sausage (or bacon if you'd rather), eggs, potatoes, bell peppers, and cheese—lots and lots of cheese. Serve them up with your favorite condiments (salsa, sour cream, jalapeños) and dig in!

INSTRUCTIONS:

1. Heat butter and oil in a medium skillet over medium–high heat. Add diced potatoes and bell peppers, and season with salt and pepper, stirring often. Cook until potatoes are golden brown, about 5 minutes. Add broth, and cook, covered, until potatoes are tender, or about 10 minutes.

2. In a separate pan, cook sausage over medium heat until brown and cooked through. Drain and return to pan. Reduce the heat to low.

3. Whisk the eggs, half–and–half (or milk), dry mustard, and seasoned salt together in a medium bowl. Gently stir in the shredded cheeses with a rubber spatula.

4. With the heat still on low, pour the egg–cheese mixture over the sausage and stir gently to combine. Continue cooking over low heat until the eggs are set and the cheese is melted.

5. To assemble, lay tortillas on a work surface and evenly distribute the sausage mixture onto tortillas. Top with potatoes. Tuck in the sides and roll up burritos. Wrap in foil to keep warm until ready to serve.

INGREDIENTS:

STREUSEL:

⅓ cup light brown sugar

⅓ cup sugar

¼ tsp. salt

1 tsp. cinnamon

½ cup unsalted butter, melted

1½ cup flour

MUFFIN:

2 cups flour

½ tsp. baking powder

½ tsp. baking soda

½ tsp. cinnamon

¼ tsp. salt

½ cup sour cream

½ cup milk

1 tsp. vanilla

½ cup butter, softened

½ cup sugar

1 egg

1 cup raspberries (fresh or frozen)

Raspberry Streusel Muffins

 25 minutes   20 minutes   Makes 12 muffins

These Raspberry Streusel Muffins have it all: brown sugary flavor, moist and fruit-packed texture, and heavy streusel topping. You won't be able to resist reaching for one (or more!) of these outrageously yummy muffins.

INSTRUCTIONS:

1. Preheat oven to 400°F. Line a 12–cup muffin tin with cupcake liners or spray with nonstick spray. Set aside.

2. To make your streusal: combine brown sugar, sugar, salt, and cinnamon in a medium bowl. Stir in melted butter, and then add in flour, using a rubber spatula to combine. Spread topping on wax paper to dry while you make your muffins.

3. Combine dry ingredients in a medium bowl: flour, baking powder, baking soda, cinnamon, and salt. Set aside.

4. In a separate small bowl, stir together sour cream, milk, and vanilla. Set aside.

5. In a large mixing bowl, cream together butter and sugar until light and fluffy. Beat in egg.

6. Stir flour mixture into creamed butter mixture alternately with sour cream mixture, just until moistened. Gently fold in the raspberries.

7. Fill the muffin cups ⅔ full. Sprinkle streusel topping evenly over tops. Bake for 18–20 minutes, or until a toothpick inserted in center comes out clean.

INGREDIENTS:

RASPBERRY LAYER:

1 large banana, sliced

1½ cups frozen raspberries

⅔ cup milk, any kind

MANGO LAYER:

1½ cups frozen mango

⅔ cup orange juice

¼ cup vanilla yogurt

Raspberry-Mango Smoothie

 10 minutes   n/a   Serves 2

My kiddo frequently asks for smoothies for an after-school snack, or as part of his dinner. Since they are full of fruit and yogurt, I'm hard-pressed to say no—and sometimes I'll add in a handful of spinach or a bit of flaxseed, and he doesn't know the difference. This version is one of our favorites, primarily because it's so colorful, but also because mangoes and raspberries are our favorite fruits.

INSTRUCTIONS:

1. Place banana slices, raspberries, and milk in the jar of a heavy–duty blender, and pulse to combine, scraping down the sides of the blender as needed. Pour mixture equally into two glasses.

2. Rinse out your blender and add mango, orange juice, and yogurt. Blend to combine, adding more orange juice if mixture is too thick. Pour mango mixture on top of raspberry mixture.

3. Top with additional mango and raspberries, if desired. Serve immediately.

Index

Cooking Measurement Equivalents

Cups	Tablespoons	Fluid Ounces
⅛ cup	2 Tbsp.	1 fl. oz.
¼ cup	4 Tbsp.	2 fl. oz.
⅓ cup	5 Tbsp. + 1 tsp.	
½ cup	8 Tbsp.	4 fl. oz.
⅔ cup	10 Tbsp. + 2 tsp.	
¾ cup	12 Tbsp.	6 fl. oz.
1 cup	16 Tbsp.	8 fl. oz.

Cups	Fluid Ounces	Pints/Quarts/Gallons
1 cup	8 fl. oz.	½ pint
2 cups	16 fl. oz.	1 pint = ½ quart
3 cups	24 fl. oz.	1½ pints
4 cups	32 fl. oz.	2 pints = 1 quart
8 cups	64 fl. oz.	2 quarts = ½ gallon
16 cups	128 fl. oz.	4 quarts = 1 gallon

Other Helpful Equivalents	
1 Tbsp.	3 tsp.
8 oz.	½ lb.
16 oz.	1 lb.

About the Author

Interestingly enough, *Ashley Whitmore* didn't grow up with an interest in cooking. In fact, she informed her mother on multiple occasions that she was not getting an advanced education so she could spend her evenings preparing meals. So here's the deal. She lucked out and got to marry her best friend. Between them, they have the cutest little Doodlebug, who is their absolute world. But balancing work and home is difficult. Sometimes impossible. She daydreams about coming home to a spotless house cleaned by a professional cleaning service, with steaming hot meals prepared by her own personal chef. But since that's not going to happen, and because she wants her son to grow up healthy and nourished by good, wholesome food, she has learned to cook. More surprising, she discovered that she actually enjoys it. She has also learned that it doesn't have to be stressful or time-consuming to create meals that are not only good for you, but also actually taste good.